Steaming to the North

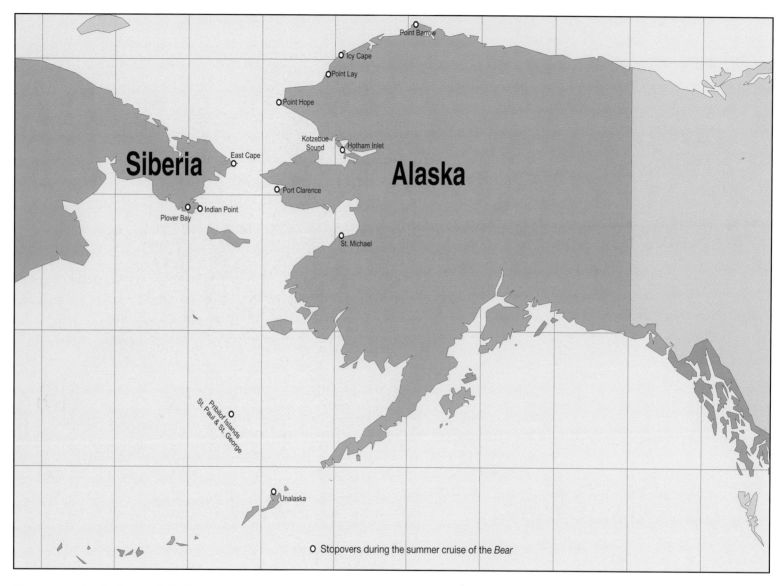

The summer cruise of the Revenue Cutter *Bear*.

STEAMING
TO THE
North

The First Summer Cruise of the
U.S. Revenue Cutter *Bear*,
Alaska and Siberia, 1886

Katherine C. Donahue and David C. Switzer

University of Alaska Press
Fairbanks

University of Alaska Press
P.O. Box 756240
Fairbanks, AK 99775-6240

Library of Congress Cataloging-in-Publication Data

Donahue, Katherine C.
 Steaming to the north : the first summer cruise of the U.S. Revenue Cutter Bear, Alaska and Siberia, 1886 / Katherine C. Donahue and David C. Switzer.
    pages cm
 Includes bibliographical references and index.
 ISBN 978-1-60223-238-9 (hardcover : alk. paper)
 1. Bear (Ship) 2. Alaska—Discovery and exploration. 3. Alaska—Description and travel. 4. Siberia, Eastern (Russia)—Description and travel. 5. Eskimos—Social life and customs. 6. Bering Sea Region—Description and travel. I. Switzer, David C. II. Title. III. Title: First summer cruise of the U.S. Revenue Cutter Bear, Alaska and Siberia, 1886.
 F908.D67 2014
 363.28'609164409034—dc23

                    2013049814

Cover design by Jen Gunderson, 590 Design
Cover photo front: Revenue Steamer *Bear* in the Bering Sea in June. Photo no. 5, McGoldrick Collection of Arctic Images, Michael J. Spinelli, Jr. Center for University Archives and Special Collections, Herbert H. Lamson Library and Learning Commons, Plymouth State University, Plymouth, NH.
Back, top to bottom: photo 26, photo 23, and photo 29, McGoldrick Collection.

This publication was printed on acid-free paper that meets the minimum requirements for ANSI / NISO Z39.48—1992 (R2002) (Permanence of Paper for Printed Library Materials).

Printed in the United States

Contents

To my colleague and dear friend, the late David C. Switzer,
whose curiosity and sense of humor kept us going,

&

To the late Charles C. McGoldrick, Jr.,
whose serendipitous find made this project possible.

Acknowledgements

The late Charles C. McGoldrick, Jr., professor at Plymouth State University in Plymouth, New Hampshire, found a set of old photographs under the porch of his house in nearby Woodstock. That discovery initiated a project that has benefited from the advice and assistance of many people. We thank Joe Muir of Black and White Photos in Portland, Maine, for giving those photographs a new life. Our colleagues at Plymouth State University have supported this project in many ways. First, we want to thank Mark Okrant, scholar of arctic tourism and cooperatives, who gave us many insights into life in the Arctic today; Virginia Fisher, exhibit designer extraordinaire; David Beronä, dean of Library and Academic Support Services; Alice Staples, archives/special collections librarian; and Susan Jarosz, archives assistant of the Herbert H. Lamson Library and Learning Commons. Kathy Melanson, Nikki Nunes, and Bryon Middlekauff of the Social Science Department helped in more ways than can be recounted here. Ross Virginia, director of the Institute of Arctic Studies at Dartmouth College; Elisabeth Smallidge, librarian at the Cold Regions Research and Engineering Laboratory in Hanover, New Hampshire; Bridget Healy and the Baxter Society of Portland, Maine; and the Norman Williams Public Library in Woodstock,

Vermont, all gave us opportunities to present this material to willing audiences. We thank the staff of the Consortium Library, University of Alaska Anchorage, for use of their photographs of Lts. Kennedy, Benham, Dunwoody, and Hassell, officers of the *Bear*. The staff of the New Bedford Whaling Museum, including Michael Lapides, curator of photography; Laura Pereira, former librarian; and Nicholas Whitman, former curator of photography, all provided ready answers to our questions. Susan A. Kaplan, director, and Genevieve LeMoine, curator, of the Peary-MacMillan Arctic Museum, Bowdoin College, offered helpful advice, as did Gregory Reinhardt of the University of Indianapolis and Terry Fifield, now retired from the U.S. Forest Service. The staff of the Rauner Special Collections Library at Dartmouth College gave us access to the many and varied books, manuscripts, and artifacts in the Stefansson Collection.

Also, we extend our deep thanks to the following scholars of the Arctic: Douglas D. Anderson, Brown University; the late Ernest S. "Tiger" Burch, Jr., Arctic Studies Center, Smithsonian Institution; Ann Fienup-Riordan, researcher and author; Lawrence D. Kaplan, director, Alaska Native Language Center, University of Alaska Fairbanks; Tom Lowenstein, author of *Ultimate Americans* and other publications on Point Hope, Alaska; and David W. Zimmerly, scholar of arctic kayaks. They helped a great deal in the identification and interpretation of the people and the material culture represented in these photographs. Igor Krupnik, curator of arctic and northern ethnology, Department of Anthropology, National Museum of Natural History, Smithsonian Institution, spent a great deal of time and effort on this project, consulting on some of the photographs and advising on the usage of terms. Without his help, many more mistakes would have been made. Alison Nordstrom, curator of photographs, and Todd Gustavson, curator of the Technology Collection of the George Eastman House International Museum of Photography and Film in Rochester, New York, provided assistance in understanding the history of photography. The people of Point Hope, including Jack Schaefer, Lily Tuzroyluke, Ray Koonuk, and Aggie Henry at Native Village of Point Hope, were welcoming and patient in answering questions. A Whiting Foundation Fellowship enabled Katherine Donahue to travel to Anchorage, Fairbanks, Kotzebue, and Point Hope, Alaska, for research on the photographs and the people and places depicted in them. Funds from the Gordon Foundation, New York, enabled us to restore the photographs. Unfortunately, David Switzer died before publication of this book, but his steady hand saw us through the revisions. William J. Donahue's patient editing has helped to remove errors and linguistic entanglements and made the *Bear*'s story come alive. Any remaining flaws are truly ours.

A Note on Terminology

The U.S. Coast Guard was officially established in 1915. Before then, the Coast Guard and its various constituents had many different names, among them the Life Saving and Lighthouse Services, the Revenue Marine Division, and the Revenue Cutter Service. We have used the term Revenue Marine Division here in order to be consistent with terminology used in 1886.

For ease in reading we have shortened the titles of ranks of officers after an initial full spelling. Although the logbook of the *Bear* used the term "3rd Lieut.," we have shortened that designation to current standards of spelling. For example, after introducing Charles Kennedy as "Third Lieutenant Kennedy" we use "Lt. Kennedy" or "3rd Lt. Kennedy."

The names of many of the places visited by the *Bear* on her first summer cruise have changed since 1886. Where necessary, in each section we have included brief discussions of those different geographical place names, using Bockstoce and Batchelder (1978) as a guide. For instance, the officers of the *Bear* used the term "Siberia" for the Chukotka Peninsula of easternmost Asia, which is now officially part of Russia's Chukotka Autonomous Okrug. For the sake of consistency with the terminology used in the original captions of the photographs and in the logbook, we have used the name "Siberia" in the title and elsewhere. However, we recognize that the term Chukotka Peninsula is used by those presently familiar with the region, and where appropriate we have used that term for what Captain Healy and his officers would have called Siberia. We have corrected the original spelling in the captions of the photographs. For Native words we have used terms and orthography recommended by the Alaska Native Language Center, University of Alaska Fairbanks. We have italicized Native words such as *umiaq* upon initial use and then adopted a normal font thereafter. Following Tom Lowenstein (2008), the name of the person in photograph 46 appears as "Ataŋauraq," although his name has been spelled in many different ways.

We know that there were significant cultural differences among the people whose images appear here. Some of those differences are readily identifiable by the clothing styles and location of the site where the photograph was taken. Wherever possible we have tried to be accurate in our description of the affiliations of these people. We have, however, frequently used the term "Native" instead of, for instance, "Siberian Yupik" or "Chukchi," because "Native" was the term used in the photographs' captions.

Introduction

In the 1970s Charles McGoldrick, a professor at Plymouth State University in Plymouth, New Hampshire, began repairs to a porch of his house in North Woodstock, fifteen miles north of Plymouth. He discovered a curious box underneath the porch. In the box were sixty-three mounted photographs. Professor McGoldrick donated the collection to the Plymouth State Social Science Department, remarking that the historians might be interested in the photographs. However, the photos were set aside for some years until the late David C. Switzer, historian and nautical archaeologist; Mark Okrant, professor of tourism management; and Katherine C. Donahue, professor of anthropology, all of Plymouth State, decided to make these unique photos accessible to more people.

The first step was to create a photo exhibit at the University's Lamson Library and Learning Commons. The opening attracted faculty, townspeople, and visitors from neighboring states. The photographs were then exhibited at the U.S. Army Cold Regions Research and Engineering Laboratory (CRREL) in Hanover, New Hampshire. As David Switzer and Katherine Donahue researched the story of the famous Revenue Cutter *Bear* and its captain, Michael Healy, the importance of the *Bear*'s first arctic patrol in 1886, reinforced by Lt. Kennedy's photographs, brought us to the second step. We contacted experts at the New Bedford Whaling Museum, at the Smithsonian, at institutions in Alaska, and elsewhere for more information on the photos and their subjects. The information gained regarding the photographs and their subject matter brought us to the third step, this book.

The years under the porch had caused the photographs to bend, and some of the images were partially obliterated by mold. A grant from the Gordon Foundation of New York City funded digital restoration carried out by Black and White Images in Portland, Maine. The result was clarity where before there was none. Unseen details became apparent (for example, see the two versions of photograph 53 on pages xiv and xv). It also became clear that the photographer had recorded a way of life long since gone.

Research revealed that these photographs had been taken on the first summer cruise of the *Bear* in the Bering, Chukchi, and Beaufort Seas, and that a Third Lieutenant Charles D. Kennedy had served on the *Bear* in 1886. If, as we believe, Kennedy was the photographer, he took some of the early photographs of the Arctic and its people. There are earlier photographs of southern Alaska, but not necessarily of arctic Alaska. Between 1877 and 1881, Edward W. Nelson of the U.S. Army Signal Corps had photographed Native people and their material culture on the Seward Peninsula and northern Alaska and what is now the Chukotka Peninsula (see his work in Hooper 1884 and in Nelson 1899). Lt. Patrick Henry Ray, also of the Signal Corps, took photographs of Native people in and around Barrow, Alaska, between 1881 and 1883 (see Ray 1885 and Murdoch 1892). A. L. Broadbent served as first assistant engineer aboard the Revenue Cutter *Corwin* and took photographs in the Arctic in 1885. His photographs can be found in the Thomas W. Benham Collection at the University of Alaska Anchorage Consortium Library. Assuming that Kennedy was indeed the photographer on the *Bear* in 1886, he was not far behind Nelson, Ray, and Broadbent.

We did not want to take at face value the information on the caption of photograph 1 as to the year and the photographer. However, we are reasonably sure that 1886 was the year for several reasons. First, 1886 was the first summer cruise of the *Bear*, and we know she was not in the western Arctic before that year. Second, photograph 4 of the *John Carver* is an image of a vessel that we know was crushed in the ice and lost in the summer of that year, after the *Bear* had seen her. The photograph could not have been taken after 1886. Third, photograph 28 of the new church at St. Michael is an image of a church that was built in 1886. The photo could not have been taken before 1886. The sharp-eyed researcher will recognize some of these photographs, for many were reproduced in Michael Healy's *Report of the Cruise of the Steamer*

"Corwin" in the Arctic Ocean in the Year 1884. However, the publication of the photographs in Healy's account of that earlier cruise does not establish that the photographs were actually taken in 1884, because that report was not published until 1889.

We are less sure that Lt. Kennedy took each one of the photographs in the McGoldrick Collection. Photograph 61 of the *Bear* had the name of the photographer W. H. Jackson attributed to it in one collection. Also, the well-known arctic photographer A. L. Broadbent was aboard the Revenue Cutter *Corwin* in 1885; however, his name does not appear on the 1886 list of crew members aboard the *Bear*. Later, Broadbent served as an engineer aboard the *Bear*, at which time he did take photographs.

Our reasons for thinking Kennedy took the photographs are as follows: The photographs comprise a complete set, and photograph 1 in the set identifies the photographer as "Lt. C. D. Kennedy." An identical set of these photographs is held in the New Bedford Whaling Museum, and the first photograph in that set also identifies Kennedy as the photographer—in penmanship different from the hand identifying Kennedy as the photographer in the McGoldrick Collection. That identical set was given to the New Bedford Whaling Museum in 1982 by Francis Kennedy and his wife of New Bedford, MA. A Kennedy family monument in St. Mary's Cemetery, New Bedford, contains the name of a Charles D. Kennedy who lived from 1858 to 1898. If that Charles D. Kennedy was on the *Bear* in 1886, he would have been twenty-eight years old at the time. We do have a photograph of him aboard the *Bear* and the age looks appropriate (see Kennedy photograph, page 10). The Kennedy Collection in New Bedford contains a photograph of a Dr. Francis M. Kennedy, who according to the Kennedy monument and a brief biography of him, was a brother of a Charles D. Kennedy. Thus these two sets each identified Lt. Kennedy as the photographer, and the New Bedford Whaling Museum's set must have passed to his family when the photographer died.

The complete Kennedy Collection consists of several sets of photographs. Most of the photographs in the first acquisition by the New Bedford Whaling Museum, in 1979, are the same as those in the McGoldrick Collection, but most are not mounted in the same way, nor do they have the caption at the bottom of the image as does the set in the second acquisition. That set, acquired in 1982 by the New Bedford Whaling Museum from the Kennedy family, is the one that is virtually identical to the McGoldrick Collection, with almost exactly the same captions and numbering system, although in different handwriting.

There are other collections with many of the same photographs as those in the McGoldrick and Kennedy Collections. Those photographs are held in the Papers of Michael A. Healy at the Huntington

53 View At Point Bay Arctic Ocean.

Photograph No. 53, unrestored.

53 View at Point Barrow Arctic Ocean.

Photograph No. 53, restored.

Library in San Marino, California; in the Thomas W. Benham Collection at the Consortium Library of the University of Alaska Anchorage; and at the Elmer E. Rasmuson Library, University of Alaska Fairbanks. While the McGoldrick photographs and those in the Kennedy Collection acquired in 1982 were very similar in their captions, some of the titles on the McGoldrick photographs contain information that conflicts with the other collections' captions. Also, some of the McGoldrick photographs have notations on the reverse in a different handwriting than the captions on the front, and occasionally the information on the reverse contradicts the information on the front. We have compared the information noted in the McGoldrick Collection with information from the three other collections (Healy, Benham, and Kennedy) in order to determine as nearly as possible the location at which each of the photographs in the McGoldrick Collection was taken. Because Captain Healy served in the Arctic longer and knew it better than many others, the captions on the photographs in the Healy Collection are thought to contain the most accurate identification. Although most of the McGoldrick captions are identical to those in the Healy Collection, where they differed we also consulted with a number of historians and ethnographers for information on clothing styles and other aspects of Native life that would identify the location or the place of origin of the people whose images were caught by the photographer.

We do not know the type of camera Kennedy used, assuming he was the photographer, but it was probably a 5" x 8" plate camera. The McGoldrick Collection photographs were most likely taken using commercially available gelatin dry plates to create the images. The exposed glass plates may have been processed on board ship or taken back to San Francisco, where they were printed and mounted, possibly by Kennedy himself as there was no studio name printed on the photos. The sepia tone of the original prints in the McGoldrick Collection is an indicator of the use of an albumen and silver nitrate mixture to create the image. The albumen (egg white) served as a binder to seal the paper on which the image was printed. The paper was then cut and pasted on a mounting board.

Kennedy had a deft eye. He recorded the legacy of the Russian presence in the Aleutians and the Alaska mainland. He recorded the growing American presence in the photographs of an army signal station in Barrow and of a little-known navy-sponsored exploring expedition. He also chose as his subjects Native people, from East Cape (Mys Dezhneva) on the Chukotka Peninsula to Barrow, Alaska, and their material culture. He photographed Native houses on both sides of Bering Strait, the Alaska way of death in the Point Hope graveyard, a dance and trade hall at Icy Cape, Alaska, and a Native summer encampment in Kotzebue Sound. When compared to the earlier photographs taken by Nelson and Ray, we see in Kennedy's work evidence of what we call the "Arctic Exchange." For example, western clothing had been adopted by some Natives. The white men on board the whaleships had adopted Native clothing. Techniques of house construction had begun to change, and trade goods were in evidence.

We have supplemented descriptions of the photographs with information from the transcript of the daily logbook entries of the *Bear*. The transcript does not include the different handwriting of the officers, because the entries were transcribed by one person after the cruise was completed. However, the officers who served on watch noted not only the weather and ice conditions but also the vessels that the *Bear* "spoke" (to "speak" meant to exchange information orally) and stopped to inspect. The logbook also indicated when Natives came on board and when passengers were taken from one place to another. The sick list was discussed, as were the supplies of coal and the amount of water taken on. In a number of cases we were able to use logbook entries to determine the date when a photograph was taken. Given the almost constant daylight of the arctic summer, the photographs could have been taken at any time, even at midnight. We have not included here every photograph in the collection, for some are quite similar to one another and others are not connected to the story of the cruise of the *Bear*.

Some mysteries remain. We do not know why the photographs were stored under Charles McGoldrick's porch, nor do we know who left them there. We would like to know more about why the numbering system on the photographs started where it did, with the whaling and trading schooner *San Jose*, because she was not the first vessel the *Bear* examined. Each one of the photographs had been numbered in a sequence that placed most of the sailing and steam whaling vessels at the beginning, then tracked the course of the *Bear* as she sailed and steamed from Unalaska to what they called Siberia (the Chukotka Peninsula), thence to Port Clarence, St. Michael, Kotzebue Sound, Point Hope, Barrow, and then back to San Francisco, enabling us to follow her cruise.

We should note that this book is in no way intended to provide a comprehensive history of Alaska during the late nineteenth century. Historians and anthropologists such as Lydia Black (2004), John R. Bockstoce (1986, 2009), Ernest S. Burch, Jr. (2005, 2006), Dorothy Jean Ray (1975), and others have given the broader perspective for understanding the complex changes occurring at the time the *Bear* sailed and steamed into arctic waters. Nor do we claim that this book provides a complete ethnographic record of the time. We have instead focused on explanations of these remarkable photographs of the first summer cruise of the *Bear*, at the same time that we put the photographs in context with brief descriptions of the history of the changing technology of whaling and of the Native peoples of the western Arctic.

The book begins with brief contextual essays on the *Bear*; her captain, Michael Healy; her officers; and her crew. It proceeds with her journey north and then follows her to Unalaska, describes her encounters with whaling and trading ships, and then moves on to ethnographic descriptions of the people and cultures as Kennedy's photographs document the path of the *Bear*.

The *Bear*

The *Bear* was built in 1874 in Dundee, Scotland, by Alexander Stephen and Sons. Before she joined the U.S. Revenue Marine Division, she had been a sealer, operating in the eastern Arctic off Newfoundland. Her reinforced bow enabled her to move through the ice when other vessels could not. She was 198 feet, 4 inches long, and had a beam of 30 feet and a draft of almost 18 feet. She had a compound expansion steam engine with two cylinders and a 30-inch stroke that produced 101 horsepower. When in the Revenue Marine Division she was armed with three six-pound rapid-fire guns (U.S. Coast Guard Cutter History, *Bear* 1885; see also Strobridge and Noble 1999).

In 1884 the *Bear* and the *Thetis*, also built by Alexander Stephen and Sons, were commissioned by the U.S. Navy to take part in the search for the ill-fated Greely Expedition. Army lieutenant Adolphus Greely and his party had been sent to Greenland and Ellesmere Island in the eastern Arctic to participate in the first International Polar Year of 1881–1883. The news that the *Bear* and the *Thetis* had found the starving survivors of this expedition captured the imagination of many Americans. The rescue was the first of events that led to the lasting admiration and affection felt for the *Bear*. On March 2, 1885, the vessel

No 5 Revenue Steamer Bear in the Behring Sea in the month of June

Photograph No. 5. Revenue steamer *Bear* in the Bering Sea in the month of June.

was transferred from the navy to the Revenue Marine Division. She then sailed and steamed around Cape Horn to San Francisco. There, on April 9, 1886, Michael Healy received orders to command the *Bear* on her first summer cruise in the Arctic.

During Washington's administration, the entity that became the Revenue Marine Division was established as a branch of the Treasury Department in order to combat smuggling and to serve as a naval auxiliary. The duties of this service soon expanded to include the Lighthouse Service, the Lifesaving Service, and the Steamship Inspection Service. With the purchase of Alaska from the Russians in 1867, the Revenue Marine's mission was expanded to include patrols along the west and arctic coasts of Alaska, into the Bering, Chukchi, and Beaufort Seas. The cutter patrols also visited the Aleutian and Pribilof Islands and easternmost Asia.

The *Bear* and her captain became the sole representative of the authority of the United States in the Arctic. In addition to stopping and inspecting vessels for illegal cargo, transporting destitute miners and prisoners, and administering justice to mutinous whaling crews, the *Bear* also provided medical and relief services for whaling crews and Natives alike. In 1897 the *Bear* assisted the Overland Expedition for the Relief of Arctic Whalers. David Jarvis, a lieutenant on the *Bear*, led the expedition, which drove reindeer north to Barrow to provide a source of food for whaling crews whose vessels had been caught in the ice. (For more on this journey, see, among others, Bixby 1965; Strobridge and Noble 1999).

The *Bear* was on arctic patrol until 1926. She made close to forty cruises north from San Francisco. In 1929 she was decommissioned by the Coast Guard and transferred to the city of Oakland, California, as a museum ship. Funds being short as the depression deepened, the city of Oakland sold her in 1932 to Admiral Richard E. Byrd. She steamed to Boston for overhaul and refitting. By then named the *Bear of Oakland*, in 1933 she was part of Byrd's second expedition to the Antarctic. She also took part in Byrd's third antarctic cruise, officially named the United States Antarctic Service Expedition, from 1939 to 1941 (U.S. Coast Guard Cutter History, *Bear*, 1885). As World War II spread in 1941, the *Bear* assisted in the evacuation of the antarctic bases.

During the war the *Bear* was refitted and served with the U.S. Navy in the Greenland Patrol as the *U.S.S. Bear*. She was on patrol during the capture of a Norwegian trawler, the *Buskoe*, which proved to be a weather ship used to drop off a crew tasked with providing meteorological reports to the Germans. In 1944 the *Bear* was stricken from the Navy list. She was sold in 1948 to be converted back to a sealer. But the

Photograph No. 6. Revenue steamer *Bear* in the ice in the month of June, Bering Sea.

price of seal skin and oil had dropped, and Albert M. Johnston, a Philadelphia entrepreneur, had different plans for her. Johnston bought and overhauled her with the intent of bringing her to Philadelphia to serve as a museum and restaurant. In March 1963, as she was being towed from Nova Scotia to Philadelphia, she took on water. Her additional weight caused the towline to part, and on March 19, 1963, she sank south of Sable Island and east of the Massachusetts coast (U.S. Coast Guard Cutter History, *Bear*, 1885).

From the Logbook

Photographs 5 and 6 show the conditions encountered by the *Bear* early in June 1886. According to the logbook of the *Bear*, after leaving the Pribilof Islands on June 1 she was frequently surrounded by ice. On June 3 the logbook ended at midnight by saying that from the crow's nest no opening in the ice was visible. By 4 PM on Sunday, June 6, they were clear of the ice, "steaming to the northward in clear water along the edge of the ice pack." At 8 PM that day they spoke the whaling bark *Dawn* from San Francisco. *Dawn* was caught in the ice, and she was not alone. From the masthead it was possible to see fourteen whaleships "all fast in the ice." The *Bear* was caught in the ice alongside the *Dawn*, but by that night she was able to work her way out to the open sea.

Michael A. Healy. *(U.S. Coast Guard's Historian's Office.)*

Captain Michael A. Healy and the Officers and Crew of the *Bear*

When the Revenue Cutter *Bear* was scheduled to begin her first patrol of Alaska and Siberian waters, Revenue Marine Division veteran Michael A. Healy was a good choice for her command. He came to the *Bear* having had plenty of experience enforcing American law on the sea. Healy was recognized as a brilliant seaman who knew the waters from Bering Strait to the Chukchi and Arctic Seas as did no other cutter captain. He was the personification of a captain of the old school, for he had four standout traits. According to an 1896 New York *Sun* article, Healy was "the ideal commander...bluff, prompt, fearless, just" (Noble and Strobridge, 2009:1). Noble and Strobridge, historians of the Coast Guard, have argued that "The *Bear* and Healy became—for all practical purposes—the Bering Sea Patrol to most people" (Strobridge and Noble, 1999:161) and that Healy was "one of this country's best Arctic navigators" (1999:181).

Michael A. Healy was born near Macon, Georgia, in 1839. He was the son of an African-American slave, Eliza, and an Irish plantation owner, Michael Morris Healy. In their biographies, O'Toole (2002) and Noble and Strobridge (2009) document the remarkable story of this family. Eliza and Michael Morris Healy had ten children who would have become slaves themselves if they had stayed in Georgia. Healy's father brought the children to New York one by one, where they were placed in the care of a business friend. They successfully passed into the white world. The girls were educated by the Catholic Church and became nuns. One left her order to marry and live in Boston. The boys were sent to grammar school and college at Holy Cross in Worcester, Massachusetts. Healy's eldest brother, James, was valedictorian at Holy Cross's first commencement, held in 1849. James later became the bishop of Portland, Maine. Another brother, Patrick, became the president of Georgetown University. But that type of education did not appeal to Michael Healy, and he ran away several times. Finally he received the blessing of his family to go to sea. He signed on as a cabin boy aboard an East India clipper in 1854. After rising quickly through the ranks, in 1865 he applied for an officer's commission with the U.S. Revenue Marine Division. He was made a third lieutenant, and married Mary Jane Roach in Boston that same year.

In 1867, the year the United States purchased Alaska, Healy sailed to the Pacific via Cape Horn on the revenue cutter *Reliance*, which was then stationed in Sitka, Alaska, through the winter of 1867–1868. Healy was appointed first lieutenant in 1870, serving on several revenue cutters. In 1874 he was sent to the new cutter *Richard Rush*, which would be based in San Francisco. He spent five years aboard her, cruising in arctic waters. In 1880 he became first lieutenant of the cutter *Corwin*, under Captain Calvin Leighton Hooper. Two years later, in 1882, a Tlingit Native died while aboard a whaling ship, and the Tlingit were thought to have taken two white men as hostages in revenge. Healy carried out the orders of Navy Commander E. C. Merriman to shell and burn the Tlingit village of Angoon. Although it was highly controversial in hindsight, this action was not reflective of Healy's usual sentiments toward Native people. Healy was promoted to captain in 1883 and assumed command of the *Corwin*. His well-written reports of

Thomas W. Benham (*Thomas W. Benham photographs, Archives and Special Collections, Consortium Library, University of Alaska Anchorage*).

Francis Dunwoody (*Thomas W. Benham photographs, Archives and Special Collections, Consortium Library, University of Alaska Anchorage*).

the *Corwin*'s 1884 and 1885 cruises demonstrate his interest in the people of the Arctic and his concern for their livelihood. Disease and starvation ravaged some areas visited by the *Corwin* and the *Bear*. In 1891, Healy, with Sheldon Jackson, the general agent for education in Alaska, bought and transported reindeer from the Chukotka Peninsula, or Siberia, to Alaska, in order to supplement the diminished caribou herd upon which many Alaskans depended for food and clothing.

Healy's treatment of officers and crew members on the *Bear* and on other ships was occasionally harsh, especially by later nineteenth century standards of conduct by captains toward crew members. Noble and Strobridge (2009) document the disciplinary action taken against Healy, both for the treatment of his subordinates and for his overindulgence in alcohol. Healy was captain of the *Bear* until 1895, when, in a disciplinary measure because of his alcoholism, he was moved to the bottom of the captains' seniority list. He was warned that if he was convicted of drunkenness again, he would be dismissed from the Revenue Marine Division. He returned to command in 1900, only to retire from service in 1903 at the mandatory age of 65. Healy died in 1904.

In the McGoldrick Collection there are no official photographs of the captain of the *Bear* or any of his officers, with one exception, noted below. Charles Kennedy's photographs are diverse in their subjects and include many aspects of Native life and culture in Alaska and on the Chukotka Peninsula, but only two show cutter crewmen at work. Nevertheless, thanks to the logbook of the *Bear*, we know the identity of those who served on her during the 1886 cruise.

Eight officers, other than Captain Michael Healy, joined the *Bear* that May. Oscar Hamlet, a Swede, was first lieutenant. He had served in that rank since 1879. We do not have a photograph of Hamlet in this section, but he does appear in a group photograph (number 40) taken at Kotzebue Sound. Images of several of the other officers on the 1886 cruise are in the Thomas W. Benham Collection, Consortium Library, University of Alaska Anchorage. Thomas W. Benham, second lieutenant, was born in England. In his photograph he is standing sideways on the deck of the *Bear*, wearing a well-fitted jacket and hat (see photograph of Lt. Benham on page 8).

Benham had held the rank of second lieutenant for four years. Third Lieutenant Francis Dunwoody, from Iowa, learned that he had qualified as second lieutenant while on this cruise. In this photograph Dunwoody, standing on the deck of the *Bear*, is dressed in fur from head to toe. The cut of the hat and parka are not of Native design, but the pants and boots are (see photograph of Lt. Dunwoody on page 9).

Third Lieutenant Charles D. Kennedy had been responsible for several rescues of shipwrecked people, off Martha's Vineyard in 1884 and then at Icy Cape, Alaska, in 1885, when serving on the *Corwin*. When the photograph was taken he was standing close to where Dunwoody's photograph was taken. His fur clothing includes a hat and parka not of Native design (see photograph of Lt. Kennedy on this page). Horace Hassell, the first assistant engineer, was from New York. Hassell is wearing a parka of Native design of the type seen in photographs 39 and 54 (see photograph of Hassell).

One photograph in the University of Alaska Anchorage collection depicts boots prominently displayed at the end of legs, attached to a man sleeping in a berth just visible in the background. The photograph is labeled "Hassell's Boots."

A. L. Churchill, chief engineer; Paul Barnes, second assistant engineer; and L. Carroll, surgeon, rounded out the complement of officers. There are no photographs of them in the Benham Collection.

There were forty crew members, including a boatswain, a carpenter, a master at arms, two quartermasters, two coxswains, thirteen

Charles D. Kennedy (*Thomas W. Benham photographs, Archives and Special Collections, Consortium Library, University of Alaska Anchorage*).

Horace Hassell (*Thomas W. Benham photographs, Archives and Special Collections, Consortium Library, University of Alaska Anchorage*).

seamen, three ordinary seamen, a cabin steward, a Japanese wardroom steward, a cook, first and second cabin boys, a machinist, five firemen, and three coal passers. A steam launch, which would provide access to shallow harbors, was stowed on board.

From the Logbook

At 12:30 PM on May 5, 1886, the crew complete and the stores stowed, the *Bear* stood out from the harbor at San Francisco. Second Lieutenant Benham reported in the logbook that the Revenue Steamer *Richard Rush* escorted them out. At 3:15 PM they passed a whistle buoy and, steering west by north, made all sail. The *Bear* was bound for Unalaska and the Bering Sea. That evening Captain Healy wrote:

> I find the blocks and running rigging, both low and aloft, to be in the worst possible condition. Orders issued to remedy their condition immediately.

Leaving light winds behind, the *Bear* sailed and steamed through increasingly foggy and rainy weather. Twelve days later, on Monday, May 17, she steamed through Unalga Pass, hauled around Priest Rock, stood up Unalaska Bay, passed over a reef, and made fast at the wharf at Unalaska.

N°12 View at Ounalaska Aleutian Islands. Alaska Com Co Building

Photograph No. 12. View of Unalaska, Aleutian Islands. Alaska Commercial Company buildings.

Unalaska

Unalaska, or Ounalaska as it was then known, is in the Aleutian chain of islands. These photos were taken at Iliuliuk Harbor, across Iliuliuk Bay from what is now called Dutch Harbor. Many of the buildings in these photographs were owned by the Alaska Commercial Company. This enterprise had taken over the Russian-American Company's extensive holdings and interests on the Aleutians, the Pribilofs, and the Alaska mainland. The Russians had been a presence in Alaska since 1732, harvesting the abundant marine resources such as sea otters and seals (see Black 2004 for discussion of the Russian presence in Alaska). Unalaska had long been the main port of call before entering the Bering Sea and the Arctic, and it was the *Bear*'s first stop. By 1886 the whaling fleet, especially the steam whaleships, would frequently put in there to take on supplies of coal and water before heading north.

On the far right of photograph 12 is the Church of the Holy Ascension, a reminder of the continuing Russian presence in Alaska. This image was made twenty years after the last Russian officials had left. The Benham Collection notes for this particular photograph say "Ounalaska, before 1885. (The date is based on the fact that the Church of the Holy Assumption was remodeled in 1885.)" However, the Church

Nᵒ 13 View at Ounalaska Alaska Commercial Com Buildings

Photograph No. 13. View at Unalaska, Alaska Commercial Company buildings.

of the Holy Ascension, its official name in English, was rebuilt in 1894–1896, not in 1885 (see Smith 1984). Not only the buildings but also the people who stayed in Unalaska were connected to Russia through birth to Native-Russian parents. These "creoles" were instrumental in the maintenance of the Russian Orthodox Church as well as in trade and other businesses (see Black 2004). Innokentii Shaiashnikov, a Native Aleut and Russian clergyman, built a church there in 1858. This church replaced an earlier one constructed by Ioann Veniaminov, who later became metropolitan of Moscow and, in 1977, was canonized as St. Innocent, enlightener of the Aleuts and apostle to America. During an inspection of Unalaska in 1880, a successor to Shaiashnikov, Bishop Nestor, thought a building to house the clergy and visiting bishop (himself) would be useful. At the time the reader of the church lived in a Native dwelling, a *barabara*, and Bishop Nestor was staying in an Alaska Commercial Company building, much to his discomfort. The Bishop's House and School were built in 1882 by the Alaska Commercial Company (Smith 1984). Visible beside the church, to the left of the porch, is a marble marker in honor of Bishop Nestor, who died at sea off Norton Sound, Alaska, in 1883. The marker was provided by the Alaska Commercial Company. The company also provided the grave marker for the Rev. Shaiashnikov, who died the same year as Bishop Nestor. The Bishop's House, photographed with someone standing in the doorway, is the large white building second from the left. The school is to the house's left, and to the right of the Bishop's House is a *barabara*, possibly that of the church reader. A 1908 map shows an "Old Customs House" and "Old Russian Garden" lying between the church and the Bishop's House.

The image in photograph 13 has peeled away from its mounting board, and some of the right side has been lost. Ships' masts are visible beyond the buildings, and Amaknak Island is in the distance. The view is from the bank of the Iliuliuk River looking past the Bishop's House toward the Alaska Commercial Company store and the company's outbuildings. A footbridge over the Iliuliuk is just visible.

Unalaska grew quickly during the late nineteenth century. By 1900 it had a hotel, a dance hall, and twelve saloons. The Russian Orthodox Church made Unalaska the administrative center for its northern Alaska parishes on the Pribilofs, at St. Michael, and on the Yukon River (Smith 1984).

The house shown in photograph 15 is a *barabara*. The word, according to Orth (1967) is of Siberian origin, from Kamchatka, probably introduced during the period of Russian occupation. The living space of these houses was partially excavated into the soil. The Aleutian barabara was rather different in outward appearance from the Native houses found on the coastline of northern Alaska, yet the house depicted here resembles those found in other northern climates such as the Hebrides or Iceland. These houses were oblong or rectangular in shape and were covered with sod and thatch. Earlier barabaras were described by observers, including the English explorer Captain James Cook, as measuring twenty feet by fifty feet. According to Nabokov and Easton (1989:205), the Russians documented some as being up to 180 feet long. In some areas, access was via the roof, with a pole or plank ladder descending to the floor below. The roof was framed with driftwood or whale bone. In this photograph, long poles, planks, and logs have been laid across the roof to keep the sod from blowing away, and there appears to be an entrance at the narrow end of the structure. A chimney is visible toward the rear, and a side annex appears to have a window. Laundry hangs on the railings outside the front entrance. The introduction of cattle to the Aleutian islands was problematic for some sod houses. The sod and grass on the roof proved too much of a temptation for the cattle, and occasionally one would fall through the roof to the floor below (Nabokov and Easton 1989:205). The railing here may not have served as a cattle fence, but it does extend around the structure.

From the Logbook

When the *Bear* put in at Unalaska on May 17 she had been at sea for twelve days. On the first day in port the crew was busy restocking coal. Over the next three days they loaded 112 tons of coal by hand. They took on 1,500 gallons of water, some for the boiler and the rest for consumption by the ship's complement. An officer checked the depths of the reef and placed ranges to guide vessels through the channel and into the harbor. The weather was squally and rainy. Since there had been problems with the rudder on the cruise north, throughout their seven-day stay in Unalaska some members of the crew made repairs to the rudder while others carried out general maintenance. The *Bear* left the coaling dock to make room for the coastal and interisland steamer *St. Paul*, mooring at a buoy in the bay. On Monday, May 24, Lt. Kennedy "gave the afternoon to the crew for a general washing of clothes." On Tuesday, May 25, upon the *Bear*'s departure at 4:10 AM, the sail sheet, the rope used to adjust a sail, parted. The crew took in the sail and spliced the sheet. They set the topsails and the *Bear* headed north to the Bering Sea.

Nº 15 Native House at Ounalaska

Photograph No. 15. Native house at Unalaska.

Cruise of Revenue Steamer Bear Season of 1886.

Capt M. A. Healy Commanding

at 6 A. M. Kennan Photographer

No 1 Whaling Schooner San Jose Behring Sea.

Photograph No. 1. Whaling schooner *San Jose,* Bering Sea.

Sailing Whaleships

Native peoples were whaling in the Bering Sea approximately three thousand years ago. During that period, someone on the southwestern side of the Chukotka Peninsula carved images on whale ivory. These carvings depicted people in an *umiaq*, or skin boat, being pulled by a whale. A drogue streamed behind in order to tire the whale (Powell 2009:27; Pringle 2008). An archaeological site at Cape Krusenstern, Alaska, contains whale bones of a similar age, but there has been disagreement as to whether the whales in question were actively hunted or were scavenged (see Giddings and Anderson 1986). Nevertheless, whaling by Alaska Natives was well established by the time the Russians and Americans arrived in Alaska.

In the eastern Arctic, Dutch and Basque whalemen were active in the sixteenth century, well before the American colonies were founded. Few of the earliest settlers in New England were skilled boat-handlers, for most of them had been farmers and merchants in England. But the prolific number of whales off the coast turned many colonists' eyes toward the sea. There was a market for whale oil in England, where it was sold for lighting and as a lubricant. The colonists quickly imitated Native whaling strategies, which involved, among other techniques, encircling whales and driving them into shallow water near the shore.

N.o 4 Whaling Bark John Carver in the ice Behring Sea afterwards Crushed

Photograph No. 4. Whaling bark *John Carver* in the ice Bering Sea; afterwards crushed.

The dead whale's blubber was rendered, or "tried," in an iron pot set over a fire. This oil was then placed in wooden casks and sold. Later, try pots were placed on vessels, and American whalers soon found whaling grounds throughout the Atlantic and Pacific Oceans.

As whalemen sailed increasing distances, sloops and schooners were replaced by larger vessels. (See photographs 1, *San Jose*, and 9, *Clara Light*, for examples of schooners.) Whaleships became factories at sea. These larger vessels could weather stormy seas while carrying large and heavy cargoes of casks filled with whale oil from distant whaling grounds. Such vessels also needed to have the most efficient sailing rig to pursue whales and to evade storms. Whalemen from Nantucket used square-rigged ships, a term for a particular type of vessel that had three masts with square sails on all masts. Barks were a later design, used by the whalemen from New Bedford. Barks also had three masts but were rigged with square sails on the forward two masts and a fore-and-aft sail on the third mast. Photographs 4 of the *John Carver*, 8 of the *Wanderer*, and 10 of the *Young Phoenix*, also known as *Young Phenix*, are of barks. The photograph of *Young Phenix* shows her painted-on gun ports. Whalers occasionally added these fake gun ports as a defensive measure in order to prevent attacks.

On June 12, 1886, the *Bear* stopped alongside the whaling and trading schooner *San Jose* (photograph 1), which was imprisoned in the ice. Schooners such as the *San Jose* that sailed in the waters of Alaska were usually built in San Francisco or other California ports. The *San Jose* was built earlier that year in Benicia, California, and had immediately headed north for whaling and trading. She was sixty-seven feet long and had a draft of only seven feet. She was seized the following year by the Revenue Steamer *Richard Rush*, Leonard G. Shepard, captain, "for violation of section 1956, R.S.," governing the unlawful taking of fur seals (*The Fur-seal and Other Fisheries of Alaska*, 1889:xxiv).

The schooner *Clara Light*, photograph 9, was built in Stellacoom, Washington. At ninety-nine feet she was longer than *San Jose*. These versatile schooners were used not only as whaleships and sealers but also as traders, bringing goods north from California. They worked as tenders as well, keeping the whaleships in supplies and returning south with oil and baleen. Schooners also traded with the Natives of Siberia (the present-day Chukotka Peninsula) and Alaska. When trading schooners were seen approaching a community, the villagers signaled to get their attention and brought their own goods out in umiaqs. The schooners usually anchored a bit off shore and dealt with the Natives on board. The Natives came away with a variety of items such as tobacco, matches, needles, cloth, knives, and axes—and sometimes illegal firearms, ammunition, and liquor. In return the schooners left with furs, baleen, and walrus ivory (Bockstoce 2009:321). It should be noted that the Russians had been trading with Alaska Natives and Siberians long before the Americans arrived. The Russians, and Natives as well, brought Asian trade goods and tobacco to Alaska. Furthermore, Native trading had been practiced long before the Russians themselves arrived. For instance, inland Natives bartered marten, wolf, and caribou furs with coastal Natives for seal, walrus, and other marine resources. Trade fairs occurred along the coast of the Chukotka Peninsula and across Bering Strait along the coastline of Alaska (see Bockstoce 2009, and discussion of photograph 43, Native camp at Hotham Inlet).

American and foreign whaleships other than schooners also traded with the Natives. As with the schooners, by the time the *Bear* patrolled the Arctic, this activity was illegal if it involved providing repeating rifles and liquor to the Natives. According to Bockstoce, trade was accompanied by sexual favors and chicanery. The whalemen sold the Natives diluted whiskey. Natives in turn deceived the whalemen by disguising damaged fox fur with rabbit skins or adding iron bars to bundles of whalebone to make them heavier (see Bockstoce 2009: 311–315, 331–339).

On July 3, 1886, the *Bear* intercepted a cargo of illegal trade goods aboard the schooner *Clara Light*, "C. B. Kustel, master, whaling." She was in the Bering Sea, not far from Norton Sound and St. Michael. Shortly after noon, the *Bear* stopped in the ice, wrote Lt. Benham, to board and examine the schooner:

> The boarding officer reported having found 20 galls whiskey in her forecastle, and the master and crew disclaiming all knowledge and ownership of the same it was thrown overboard. 8000 Winchester cartridges found in the same place were given in charge of the master and his receipt taken therefor.

Since quarters were tight and the liquor and ammunition would have been obvious, no one on the *Bear* credited the *Clara Light*'s version of the story. Benham went on to say that

> [t]he crew nearly all of whom were interested volunteered the information that 26 Bbls [barrels] of whiskey + 2 cases of arms had been thrown overboard upon the approach of the Cutter.

After that episode, the *Clara Light* did not have a long career as a trader, for she was abandoned in the ice north of Point Franklin later that season.

Nº 8 Whaling Bark Wanderer in the Behring Sea

Photograph No. 8. Whaling bark *Wanderer* in the Bering Sea.

No 9 Whaling Schooner "Clara Light" in the ice Behring Sea

Photograph No. 9. Whaling schooner *Clara Light* in the ice, Bering Sea.

The *John Carver* (photo 4) and the *Wanderer* (photo 8) and *Young Phenix* (photo 10) represented the end of the era of the sailing whaleships. When the photograph of *John Carver* was taken she had been in active service as a whaler for twenty years. Built in Searsport, Maine, in 1857, the bark *John Carver* shipped out of New Bedford to the arctic whaling fields in 1866. By 1886 she was sailing out of San Francisco, as were many New Bedford whaleships, for in that year at least forty-four western arctic whaleships used San Francisco as a home port. Two years later, *Young Phenix* was lost off Point Barrow (see Bockstoce 2006:66). By the 1920s there were only three American sailing vessels that hunted whales. One was the *Wanderer* (photograph 8). Built in Mattapoisett, Massachussetts, in 1878, she served in the sailing whaler fleet for forty-six years. In August 1924 she was making her way from New Bedford to Nantucket to pick up crew members, but hurricane force winds blew her onto the shoals off Cuttyhunk Island. Although all hands were saved, the *Wanderer* was a total loss.

From the Logbook

The logbook of the *Bear* tells some of *John Carver's* story, and that story is a reminder of the perils of arctic whaling: unpredictable drift ice could lead to an untimely end. In photograph 4 the *John Carver* is icebound and, as the caption relates, "afterwards crushed." Lt. Kennedy apparently was standing on the ice when he took this photograph. On June 9, 1886, the *Bear's* location was reported as in the Bering Strait and "in the Ice Pack." At 12:20 PM that day Lt. Benham noted that she "stopped alongside of the whaling Bark *John Carver*." Twenty minutes later the *Bear* went ahead and at 3:30 reached open water, then again worked her way through the ice pack near the schooner *Hamilton*. Three weeks later, on July 2, the *Bear* was in the Bering Sea, where she made for St. Lawrence Island and on the way stopped to inspect the *Hamilton*. Two officers from the *Bear* boarded the schooner, and returned with the news that

> A. Rider, the master of the *Hamilton*, reported the loss of the *John Carver* in the
> ice off St. Lawrence Isld. + the probable loss of the whaling bark *Hunter* on or
> near the Pinnock Rocks.

According to the November 23, 1886, edition of the *Whalemen's Shipping List*, published in New Bedford, the *Hunter*, with Bernard Cogan, master, survived. She arrived in San Francisco on November 14, 1886. But the August 17, 1886, edition of the same newspaper reported that the *John Carver* was lost on June 21, north of St. Lawrence Island (*Whalemen's Shipping List*). On July 18, when the *Bear* was near Cape Krusenstern, north of Kotzebue, Alaska, she spoke the steam schooner *Alliance*, James McKenna, master, "and found that he had the wreck of the Whaling Bark *John Carver* in tow of the boats." Later while at Point Barrow, the logbook of the *Bear* carried this entry for August 14:

> At 11 Stmr. *Alliance*, McKenna, came into the anchorage and reported the wreck
> of the whaling Bark *John Carver* laying E.S.E. 6 or 7 miles from C. Thomson
> with lower masts above water.

Nº 10 Whaling Bark Young Phoenix, Arctic Ocean Capt. W.M. Barnes Mast

Photograph No. 10. Whaling bark *Young Phoenix*, Arctic Ocean, Capt. W. M. Barnes, master.

Nª 2 Whaling Steamer Thrasher Behring Sea Nov

Photograph No. 2. Whaling steamer *Thrasher*, Bering Sea.

Steam Whaleships

In the 1880s, a new type of American whaleship appeared in the waters of the Bering Sea. When at anchor and seen from a distance these auxiliary powered whaleships resembled the sailing bark-rigged whaleships that had been chasing bowhead whales for the past forty years. What made the newcomers different was a smoke stack that vented the smoke from a boiler that powered a steam engine that turned a two-bladed propeller. Some of the steamers were powered by a new type of two-cylinder engine, known as a compound engine. This engine used steam from the boiler only once to activate both pistons, creating 200 to 300 horsepower. Compound engines were more expensive than the single-cylinder type; however, their efficient use of coal fuel paid off. In addition to the smoke stack, a sharp-eyed person would have noted that the bows of steam whaleships were designed after the sharp and graceful bows of clipper ships; unseen were timber reinforcements in the bow that allowed these vessels to steam through six-inch ice in order to flee oncoming drift ice that could entrap and crush sailing whaleships (Bockstoce et al. 1977:64).

The American whaling industry had been slow to embrace vessels with auxiliary power. This apparent reluctance was largely due to the fact that the whaling fleet had done so well without it. American

Nº 7 Whaling Steamer Grampus Behring Sea, Looking for Whales

Photograph No. 7. Whaling steamer *Grampus*, Bering Sea, looking for whales.

whalemen had excelled at hunting whales in the South Atlantic and Pacific Oceans, where there was no threat of becoming ice-bound and crushed. The Scots, however, had built steam-powered auxiliary sailing vessels used to hunt seals in waters off Greenland since the 1850s. They had come to appreciate the greater maneuverability provided by an engine while operating in eastern arctic waters choked with ice (Baker 1977:63; Bockstoce 1986:209–210). The *Bear*, built in Scotland as a sealer in 1874, was an example of such a vessel. However, in the eastern Arctic, commercial exploitation of bowheads had occurred since the mid-1500s. As a result, the bowhead stock there was increasingly in decline (Allen and Keay 2006). Elsewhere in the Atlantic and Pacific, sperm and right whales were also becoming more difficult to find. When the American captain Thomas Roys sailed the bark *Superior* north through Bering Strait in the summer of 1848, he discovered bowhead whales in the Bering and Chukchi Seas. Thus began a new and final chapter in the story of American whaling. Roys's discovery, according to Bockstoce, was "the most important whaling discovery of the nineteenth century" and "one of the most important events in the history of the Pacific" (1986:24). This was new, untouched territory for the American whalemen, or for anyone except the Natives.

American whalemen used to southern waters had to learn new techniques for hunting bowhead whales. The bowhead, *Balaena mysticetus*, is in the same family, Balaenidae, as the right whale. Slow and abundant in their feeding grounds, the Bering Sea bowheads wintered in the Bering Sea and then moved north to the Chukchi and Beaufort Seas in the spring. When bowheads were chased they sought safety under the ice. Their blubber could be as much as two feet thick, and a single whale when tried out could fill 100 thirty-one-gallon casks of oil (Bockstoce et al. 1977:17). Also, instead of teeth, these whales had valuable baleen, a keratinous substance that hangs from the whale's upper gum in plates. These plates are used as filters while feeding on krill and copepods, the basic food of toothless whales (see Lee 1983:10). Although baleen had been harvested from right whales in the Atlantic and Pacific, the amount of baleen per right whale was minimal compared with that of a bowhead.

As Bockstoce et al. (1977) and Lee (1983:10) noted, baleen was the plastic of the day. An 1885 report of the U.S. commissioner of fisheries described a patent for rendering baleen, or whalebone, as it was called, into a plastic substance by dissolving baleen in an alkali solution (*Report* 1887:1091). It was highly prized for buggy whips, hoop skirts, parasol frames, and the corset stays that women wore to achieve fashionably narrow waists. When petroleum was discovered in Pennsylvania in 1859, it began to replace whale oil for lighting. Whalers increasingly focused on the profits to be gained from baleen. Bockstoce et al. (1977) includes a copy of an advertisement printed in 1882 by W. M. Lewis, a New Bedford importer of "Whalebone (and) Oil." Note that "whalebone" precedes "oil," indicating, it appears, that whalebone was by then considered more important than whale oil.

Within thirty years after Thomas Roys's discovery, a significant number of American sailing whaleships had been caught and crushed in the western arctic pack ice and lost. Ice floes driven by contrary winds often made it impossible for sailing whaleships to escape the wind-driven ice. This had been the situation that doomed sailing whaler fleets in 1871 and 1876, causing the loss of forty-two vessels in all (Bockstoce 1986:101–107). These disasters led to the adoption in 1880 of steam whaleships in the western arctic whaling fleet (Bockstoce et al. 1977:17, 18). Steam whaleships with their extremely sturdy hull construction and heavily reinforced bows could churn through six-inch ice while engaging their propellers to avoid dangerous ice floes (see Bockstoce et al. 1977:67). By the end of the nineteenth century, steam whaleships wintered in the ice for months, a practice that had been followed in the eastern Arctic since the 1850s (see Ross 1985). The vessels emerged from the ice intact and ready to hunt when the whales returned to their summer feeding grounds. The *Thrasher* overwintered twice, the *Grampus* four times. The *Grampus* appears in an 1894 aerial view of whaleships wintering over at Herschel Island. In a painting by John Bertoncini ("Whaleships in Winter Quarters at Herschel Island, 1893–4") seven steam whaleships are snugly iced in. Smoke billows fore and aft from each vessel. Piles of coal and other supplies are visible on shore, and the crews are playing soccer and baseball (Bockstoce et al. 1977:87, 94).

Nevertheless, even with the ability to pursue the bowhead, steam whaleships could not save the whaling industry from its demise. New technology, in the form of explosive bombs fired from guns and lances, increased the kill success rate (Bockstoce 1986:69). The high costs of construction plus the increasing price of coal made operation of the steam whaleships expensive, even though the whalemen quickly utilizaed coal deposits in Alaska (see the discussion of photograph 52, landing place at Cape Lisburne). Then too there was a decline in demand for whale products. Not only had the introduction of petroleum replaced the demand for whale oil, but the changing whims of ladies' fashion also reduced the demand for baleen. Corset stays were increasingly made of spring steel. It was petroleum and spring steel that helped save the whales from extinction. Had steam power been introduced to western arctic whaling earlier, it is possible that the bowhead whale population would have been drastically depleted before the end of the century. As it was, Bockstoce and Botkin (1983) have demonstrated that the western arctic bowhead population was in decline by the beginning of World War I, and pelagic whaling there came to an end.

The *Belvedere* (photograph 11), built in 1880, and the *Thrasher* (photograph 2), built in 1883, were both launched at Bath, Maine. Ultimately, twelve steam whaleships were built in Bath, and the American steam whaling fleet eventually numbered thirty vessels, including those of the Pacific Steam Whaling Company (Bockstoce et al. 1977:77–102). The *Grampus* had been built in 1874 in East Boston by the Atlantic Works, but not for the whaling trade. She was originally commissioned as the first *Richard Rush* of the Revenue Marine Division. A steam barkentine, this was the vessel on which Michael Healy had served early in his arctic career. She was later purchased by the Pacific Steam Whaling Company. In 1886 she was on her first whaling trip, under the command of Henry G. Dexter, heading north together with her new sister ship, the steamer *Thrasher*.

From the Logbook

The *Grampus* and the *Thrasher* were seen and spoken by the *Bear* during her patrol. On June 16, 1886, the *Bear* was off the Chukotka coast at Indian Point, or Mys Chaplina. By 8:45 AM the *Bear* was underway, and at 11:00 she stopped and spoke the steam whaling bark *Thrasher*. Second Lt. Benham reported that the *Bear* went ahead again at 11:45 AM, then stopped and spoke the *Grampus*. Charles Brower, who later settled in Barrow, Alaska, reported this encounter in his memoirs, the best known of which is *Fifty Years below Zero* (1947; see note in references). Brower was on the northward-bound *Grampus* when his vessel encountered the steamer *Thrasher*, also with the Pacific Steam Whaling Company. Brower and some of his fellow crew members walked six miles across the ice to the *Thrasher*, where they "gammed," or visited, with members of the *Thrasher*'s crew (Brower 1947:74–75). Later the *Bear* encountered the *Thrasher* several times during the summer. On July 11 the *Thrasher* was at Port Clarence, as were a number of other whaleships. The *Bear* saw the *Thrasher* again on August 14 at Point Barrow. Encounters such as these were frequent, as the whaling fleet slowly moved north with the breaking ice.

Despite the improved design of the steam whaleships, the ice often prevailed. In 1901, the *Grampus* was finally caught by the ice off Point Barrow. She was beached and condemned there (Bockstoce et al. 1977:94). The *Thrasher* became a trader. She subsequently burned and sank off the Aleutians in 1921 (Bockstoce et al. 1977:87). After twenty-five whaling voyages, the longest career of any other steam whaler, the *Belvedere* also became a trader. In 1919 she was caught in the ice northwest of East Cape, or Mys Dezhneva, Chukotka, and crushed (Bockstoce et al. 1977:78).

N° 11 Whaling Steamer Belvedere off Cape Lisbourne Arctic Ocean

Photograph No. 11. Whaling steamer *Belvedere* off Cape Lisburne, Arctic Ocean.

Nᵒ 18 View of Seals at the Island of St Paul Behring Sea

Photograph No. 18. View of seals at the island of St. Paul, Bering Sea.

The Bear *at the Pribilof Islands*

The Pribilof Islands are in the Bering Sea some two hundred miles north of Unalaska. St. Paul and two smaller islands, Walrus and Otter, lie about forty miles north of St. George Island. This group of islands was named for Gavriil Pribilof, a Russian who in the mid-eighteenth century discovered the commercial potential of the large fur seal colonies found there. Each summer northern fur seals, *Callorhinus ursinus,* move north to the Pribilofs. There they give birth and feed their pups. The islands had been uninhabited until the Russians enslaved members of the Aleut population and forced them to move north to work in the sealing industry.

When the Russians departed in the nineteenth century, they left behind the Aleuts, their houses, a Russian Orthodox church, and a cemetery. The United States government quickly assumed control of the properties and seal herds because they represented a lucrative resource. The government leased the commercial enterprise to the Alaska Commercial Company, which detailed agents to St. Paul and St. George Islands. The Revenue Marine Division patrolled the waters around the Pribilofs and inspected vessels nearby to ensure that seals, especially female seals, were not taken illegally. The Revenue Marine also

Nᵒ 19 Grave Yard at St Pauls Islands. Greek Church —

Photograph No. 19. Graveyard at St. Paul Island; Greek church.

contributed manpower to help in monitoring the seal population. For instance, in 1885 Lt. Benham was sent ashore from the *Corwin* for several weeks, relieving Lt. John Cantwell of the Revenue Marine Division, who proceeded to Kotzebue Sound to explore the Kobuk River.

From the Logbook

These photographs were taken in May or in mid-September, for the *Bear* visited there twice. She first arrived on May 26, twenty-four hours after leaving Unalaska. She put in at St. George Island, where the Alaska Commercial Company's agent and employees came on board, stayed for about an hour, and then left. The *Bear* then made her way to St. Paul Island, where she stayed for two days. Photograph 18 shows some of the thousands of seals on the shoreline of St. Paul. The graveyard in photograph 19 was established by the Russian Orthodox Church. (The terms "Greek" and "Russian" Orthodox were often used interchangeably.) The Church of Sts. Peter and Paul stands just beside the graveyard but is not in the view here. The houses below the graveyard were used by the Alaska Commercial Company personnel. An 1890 map drawn by Henry Elliott shows about eighty buildings, including the church, a school, a salt house, shop, barn, and company store (Elliott 1890). There were two large killing grounds indicated on the map. The seals were herded away from the water to these killing grounds and then clubbed to death.

According to the logbook of the *Bear*, she returned to the Pribilofs on September 10 on her way south. The agents and personnel again came on board. The crew set to work painting the port side of the hull and iron rails. On September 11, Lt. Kennedy wrote of a visit to St. George Island:

> ...gentle breeze from E.S.E. and partly cloudy. Crew painting forwd sky-
> lights. 1st Lieut. O. C. Hamlet visited the settlement officially. Other officers
> of the vessel and of the Stoney party socially.

The Stoney party, led by Lt. George Stoney, had been on a naval exploring expedition up the Kobuk River in Alaska. That expedition is described more fully in the explanation accompanying photograph 40.

Nº 20. Views at Indian Point Russian Siberia, "Home at Last"

Photograph No. 20. View at Indian Point, Russian Siberia. "Home at Last."

The Chukotka Peninsula, Siberia

This group of photographs was taken on the Chukotka Peninsula, in easternmost Asia. The region, referred to at the time as "Siberia" by the Americans, is now part of the Russian Chukotka Autonomous Okrug. It is bounded by the Bering Sea to the south, the Chukchi Sea to the north, and Bering Strait to the east. East Cape (photograph 27) was named by Captain James Cook. Now Mys Dezhneva, it is the easternmost point of that peninsula. Indian Point (photographs 20, 23, and 24), known in Siberian Yupik as Ungaziq and to the Russians as Mys Chaplina, is a long spit of land sheltered by mountains. It was frequented by whaleships. Plover Bay, or Bukhta Provideniya, also provided shelter for whaleships and traders.

In photograph 20, "Home at Last," the scene has been staged so that a female passenger is seated on a dogsled. Six dogs are harnessed in a single line. Note the snow in this photograph. It was probably taken less than two weeks before the summer solstice. In the near distance is a large skin tent supported by poles and in the far background are two steam whaleships. The smoke suggests that steam pressure was being kept up to ensure the steam whalers would be able to move away from the ice that was present even in June (Bockstoce, pers. comm., March 3, 2013. The narrow vertical objects standing in the snow behind

No 22. Native Houses at Plover Bay Russian Siberia, Plebian Neighborhood

Photograph No. 22. Native houses at Plover Bay, Russian Siberia: plebian neighborhood.

the house and to its left are whale bone. There are three separate ceremonial clusters of these bones, testimony to the importance of whales and whaling to the Native community.

According to the logbook, the *Bear* made several stops along the Chukotka Peninsula, in June and again in September 1886. Healy would have known that American whaleships and trading ships were either caught in the ice in the Bering Sea or were in the harbors of what the Americans called Plover Bay, Indian Point, and East Cape. Siberian Yupik and Chukchi people brought their dog teams and reindeer caravans to meet these whaleships and traders, arriving first in mid-March, and they continued to arrive as long as the vessels were there (Bockstoce 2009:336). Edward Nelson, the naturalist and ethnographer who was with the U.S. Army Signal Corps, came to Plover Bay, or Bukhta Provideniya, on the *Corwin* in 1881. He observed,

> This village is not very populous, and through the introduction of whisky and of various diseases by the whalers, who call here every season, the Eskimo at this point are in a fair way to become extinct (Nelson 1899:259).

In 1885, Captain Healy reported that

> At Cape Tchaplin [Indian Point] Indians visited the vessel in an intoxicated condition, and the *omalik* [chief] informed us that about fifty barrels of rum were concealed on shore, which had been traded for by his people with American whaling vessels (Healy 1887:15).

The leader at Indian Point was noteworthy. The U.S. Coast and Geodetic Survey schooner *Yukon* stopped at Indian Point in 1880. The author of a report from the *Yukon* to the *New York Times*, perhaps the surveyor and naturalist William Healey Dall, wrote that whaleships took Native men north from Indian Point to assist with whaling in the Chukchi Sea and the Arctic Ocean at the beginning of the season in the spring and then returned the men at the end of the season. He went on to say that

> The Indian Point men never lose an opportunity to go aboard a vessel; they will follow one for hours, paddling with all possible haste, and never give up the chase as long as they gain the least bit.... One of the men called himself the chief; he wore a parka made of a very pretty piebald skin of tame reindeer.

> We found it hard to trade for such piebald skins, as the natives invariably prize them highly ("Ten Days in the Arctic" 1880:2).

The chief was probably Quwaaren, also spelled Koara (Lee and Reinhardt 2003) and Goharren (Bockstoce 1986, 2009). This man was a powerful and wealthy trader. Bockstoce (1986:195–198) wrote that Quwaaren had acquired his wealth through canny, occasionally deceitful, barter. One incident concerning him occurred later in the *Bear*'s first summer cruise. On August 18, 1886, the *Bear* was between Wainwright and Cape Lisburne on the northern Alaska coast when she spoke the schooner *Henrietta*. Third Lt. Dunwoody wrote that at 7:40 PM they

> stopped engine + hove to + communicated with her + sent an officer to board her. Proved to be the schr. "Henrietta" of San Francisco, Dexter master. Captain Dexter reported having sold his vessel to a native chief at Cape Tchaplin, Siberia, for 4000 lbs whalebone and now seeking a vessel to take his crew and whalebone to San Francisco.

This Native chief would have been Quwaaren/Goharren. A photo of him and his son are to be found in Bockstoce 1986:198 and 2009:343. On August 29, 1886, Quwaaren/Goharren lost the *Henrietta* to the Russians, who claimed he did not have the authority to use her in Russian waters. Five of the American crew members still aboard had to make their way home by way of Vladivostok and Nagasaki (see *Papers Relating to the Foreign Relations of the United States* 1888:492–493). Both the schooner and the goods she carried were confiscated (Bockstoce 1986:198–199).

The Plover Bay houses in photograph 22 are examples of double-arch tents (Lee and Reinhardt 2003). The roof slopes to the rear; the entrance is to the front. These buildings were primarily summer houses. Lee and Reinhardt (2003:148) suggest that they were made of walrus hide, probably rubbed with fat in order to resist water and to let in daylight. Large stones weigh down the sides. Hanging from the roof poles of the third tent from the right is an inflated sealskin, commonly used as a float to keep harpooned animals or disabled kayaks from sinking.

In photograph 23, three Indian Point houses are lined in a row. A group of fourteen or more people stand before them, two on a sled. One woman wears pigtails, and in the back is a man with a non-Native hat. A man facing him, with his back to the photographer, wears a long coat or cloak. Despite the

No 73 Deer Skin house Indian Point Russian Siberia,

Photograph No. 23. Deer skin house, Indian Point, Russian Siberia.

Nᵒ 24 Natives of Indian Point taken on board Stmr Bear

Photogrpah No. 24. Natives of Indian Point, taken on board steamer *Bear.*

caption, the houses were probably made from walrus skin. John Murdoch noted that in Siberia (the Chukotka Peninsula) people were abandoning the semisubterranean houses they had used in favor of the "double-skin tent of the Chukches" (1892:78). The abandoned semisubterranean houses were then used to cache food and supplies, much as the Natives of northern Alaska were to do with their old semisubterranean houses.

In photograph 24, eight visiting men and women in parkas are grouped at the *Bear*'s main mast. In his report on the 1885 cruise of the *Corwin*, Healy wrote that

> Every vessel cruising in the Arctic is visited by the natives, and inflicted with
> their presence. They often remain twenty-four or even forty-eight hours at a
> time on board; and frequently depend almost entirely on the vessels visited
> for their food during their stay (Healy 1887:16).

The Benham Collection identifies the photograph as taken "Off Icy Cape" (in Alaska), and the Healy Collection says they are "Natives of East Cape, Siberia." Here they are identified as being from Indian Point. The parkas worn by three women on the left appear to be cloth, and the next person is wearing a seal gut parka with epaulets. Sitting to the right of the group is a sailor in his uniform, paying no attention to the photographer or the group being photographed.

Photograph 27, titled "View on the Ice at East Cape. Hunting Expedition," was apparently taken at East Cape and labeled as members of a hunting party. There are at least sixteen people, fifteen dogs, and five sleds. Yet there appear to be no hunting weapons. The caption in the Healy Collection reads "Indian Trading Party on the Ice, East Cape, Siberia." The group may well have been out on the ice for trading, since the logbook indicates that Natives boarded the *Bear* a number of times while she was off East Cape.

From the Logbook

In June there was still enough ice to keep the whaleships from moving into the Chukchi Sea in pursuit of the migrating bowhead whales. The *Bear* became caught in the ice off shore, as did several other vessels. She was in the ice pack from June 8 to June 13. During the 8 AM to noon watch on June 13, 1886, Lt. Benham reported that "Qr. (Quartermaster) Mr. Johnson was injured at the wheel while backing through the ice." Johnson was placed on the sick list and remained there for six weeks, until July 25. On June 14 the *Bear* was underway again and she visited Indian Point from June 14 to 16. On the sixteenth, Lt. Kennedy reported that the steamers *Orca* and *Mary and Helen* left the port. The *Bear* got under way, but two hours later stopped and spoke the steam whaling barks *Thrasher* and *Grampus*. Charles Brower, then aboard the *Grampus*, had said the two whaling crews visited each other in May. The two vessels apparently had perforce stayed on into June, when the *Bear* saw them. *Grampus* and other whaleships had no luck finding whales, but the *Thrasher*, according to Brower, took two bowhead whales (Brower mss. and 1947:75).

The *Bear* bore for East Cape, stopping to speak the whaling steamer *Narwhal*, Martin Van Buren Millard, master, and then spoke the steamer *Alliance*, James McKenna, master. The logbook shows that the *Bear* was at East Cape on June 17 and 18. Then, between noon and 4 PM on the 18th, Lt. Benham noted that the *Bear* "worked clear of the ice and steamed towards the Diomedes," islands midway between Asia and Alaska. By 10 PM they were off Cape Prince of Wales, Alaska, where Lt. Benham reported they "slowed again to allow Natives to visit the vessel. Went ahead fast at midnight course south, thick fog and fresh SE breeze."

The *Bear* did not visit Plover Bay until September 6. She was on her return trip, heading south to Unalaska and home to San Francisco. She rounded the spit entrance to Plover Bay and anchored. The officers took a series of observations to verify the chronometers' accuracy as well as the variation of the compass. The hands were set to scrubbing the outside of the ship, and the surgeon went onshore to provide medical assistance to the Natives. The *Bear* got underway at 4:50 the following morning and set a course for St. Lawrence Island.

No 24 View on the Ice at East Cape   Hunting Expedition

Photograph No. 27. View on the ice at East Cape. Hunting expedition.

Nº 28 New Church @ St Michaels Alaska

Photograph No. 28. New church at St. Michael, Alaska.

St. Michael, Alaska

Mikhailovskii Redoubt, or St. Michael, was established by the Russian-American Company in 1833. Conveniently, it was close to the mainland ("separated by a narrow, crooked, tidal slough" according to Lt. David H. Jarvis [1900:37]) and yet close enough to deep water in Norton Sound to allow ships to anchor nearby. Sixty miles northeast of the shallow waters of the delta of the Yukon River, St. Michael became an important port and depot for fur traders who ventured up the Yukon River into Alaska's interior (see Bockstoce 2009). Steamboats moved goods between St. Michael and villages up the Yukon River until competition from railroad service in the interior rendered the steamboats no longer useful and St. Michael less important as a depot.

According to Dorothy Jean Ray, the old chapel, visible to the right in photograph 28, was built in 1842 by the Russian-American Company (1975:123). In 1844 Grigorii Golovin, a Russian Orthodox priest, was ordered to finish the chapel, and it was formally dedicated in December of that year (Ray 1975:208; Smith 1984). The building to the left, the Church of the Holy Protection, had just been erected. In this photo, it appears that the cross had been removed from the old chapel and placed on the new church, where

Nº 30. View at St Michaels Alaska

Photograph No. 30. View at St. Michael, Alaska.

it was supported by guy wires. The *Bear* put in at St. Michael twice that summer, in early July on her way north and in late August as she was heading home to San Francisco. Given the fact that the new church at St. Michael looks completed, it is probable that many of the photographs were actually taken between August 28 and September 4.

St. Michael was located between two Native villages. Lt. Zagoskin (1967:100), who travelled to St. Michael in 1842, reported that Tachik/Taciq, which had once served as a Native meeting place for trade goods, was close to the fort. Atkhvik/Atuik, to the northwest, was near Cape Stephens and what is now Stebbins, Alaska. In photograph 30 there is a sod-roofed wooden structure to the left. Entrance to these houses would have been from either a covered surface passage or from a tunnel, or in the summer as the ground thawed and water filled the passage, from a side door or hole. The exterior was made of horizontally laid logs, with a sod roof overhead. One of Edward Nelson's photographs of Tachik, taken in 1877, shows six men standing on the roof of a men's house or *qasgiq* (see Nelson 1877). To the right in photograph 30 there is a drying rack for meat such as bearded seal or fish. Adjacent to the rack is another structure with a sled and an umiaq framework on the roof. The umiaq's skin covering has been removed. Kayaks and umiaqs were placed on racks, especially if they were covered with skin, because these racks also protected drying meat and the skin covers of kayaks and umiaqs from predatory animals.

Eight wall tents line the shore at St. Michael in photograph 32. One tent to the far right is made of striped cloth. Two umiaqs are propped up on their gunwales and kayaks are drawn up on the beach. Between the second and the third tent on the left, a large hide is stretched on a rack. A man sits in front of the large white tent on the right, and to the right of him, near the striped tent, another man is holding a large bundle that may contain hides. On his visit in June 1881, John Muir described these settlements of tents belonging to traders and Natives who brought furs from different outposts on the lower Yukon River (1917:81–83). The goods were stored in warehouses at St. Michael, awaiting the arrival of the Alaska Commercial Company's ships and other trading ships in the summer.

From the Logbook

The officers of the *Bear* first set course for St. Michael on Saturday, June 19, when they were off Cape Prince of Wales. Lt. Dunwoody noted that from midnight to 4 AM they were "steaming along edge of ice pack. Stopping at intervals to allow natives to come on board." Later that day they stopped off Sledge Island, again to let Natives come on board. They then headed southeast for St. Michael. At midnight they rounded Cape Nome and on Sunday, June 20, came to off St. Michael, where they dropped anchor in the ice. But at 8 PM, caught in the drift ice, the *Bear's* anchor "commenced to drag under the great pressure." Lt. Kennedy had the 8 PM to midnight watch. He noted that the weather was overcast and raining.

> At 9 vessel rapidly dragging + under full pressure of steam ahead not being able to get the anchor. buoyed + slipped the cable at 18 fms in 3 ¼ fms water.... Steamed ahead through the ice.

Having lost an anchor, the *Bear* left Norton Sound, steaming and sailing to St. Lawrence Island then towards East Cape, Chukotka, and on to Hall's Island where they took on water. They did not return to St. Michael until Sunday, July 4. By then the ice was gone, and the officers and crew of the *Bear* celebrated the Fourth of July. Between 4 and 6 PM, with a moderate southwest wind, they came to off St. Michael in three and a half fathoms of water. They then "dressed ship and fired a salute of 21 guns, in honor of the day." On Monday, July 5, between 4 and 8 AM, they sent an officer out to search for the lost anchor. Lt. Dunwoody noted that they "also took azimuths on shore + determined the variation of the compass to be East 22 degrees, 15'30"." On the next watch, from 8 AM to noon, they sent out two boats and two officers to sweep for the anchor with a weighted line secured to each boat. During the following watch, between noon and 4 PM, again two boats, officers, and crew continued sweeping and dragging for the anchor. At 4:30 PM Lt. Benham observed that the "boats returned unable to find the anchor on account of the soft bottom of mud." The search was abandoned. The following day, July 6, the crew "performed the usual morning duties" and then cleaned the boats. The *Bear* headed out into the Bering Sea, not to return to St. Michael until August 28.

Photograph No. 32. Views at St. Michael, Alaska.

Photograph No. 35. Native in his kayak belonging to St. Michael, Alaska.

Kayaks at St. Michael

The solo kayaker in photograph 35 is wearing a fur parka with a hood. He is sculling with a single-bladed paddle and is seated well down inside the cockpit. Some material, possibly a gutskin or cloth parka, is wedged behind his back. At the rear is a handgrip for ease in carrying the kayak. The handgrip was formed from an extension of the aft stringers, the longitudinal framing that extended from bow to stern (Zimmerly 2000). Several styles of kayaks were made in the area between Norton Sound and Nunivak Island to the south. The most obvious distinguishing features can be seen in the bow and stern. The kayaks in photograph 36 represent two different styles. The three on the left have beak-like bows, formed from extensions of the stringers. These also functioned as handles for carrying the craft or pulling it onshore. The sterns are also similar to the one in photograph 35. These kayaks were found through-out the St. Michael and Norton Sound area (see Graburn et al. 1996:189, 191 for kayak models of similar design). The kayak on the right with the round hole at the bow is a variant of the other three, but most likely it is also from St. Michael (Zimmerly, pers. comm., November 11, 2012; also see Fienup-Riordan 2007; VanStone 1989; and Zimmerly 1979 for detailed descriptions of kayak construction to the south of

N.º 36 Natives in Kyaks at St Michaels Alaska

Photograph No. 36. Natives and kayaks at St. Michael, Alaska.

St. Michael). Adney and Chapelle (1964:197) proposed that the round hole in the bow served several purposes. It was a handgrip, and it also resembled a seal's head, with the hole representing the eyes of the seal. Kayakers often carried two different sizes of single-bladed paddles, large and small, and this appears to be the case in photograph 36. Long, narrow blades were more quiet and they ensured less wind resistance (Fienup-Riordan 2007:104).

Kayaks were used for hunting seals, walruses, birds, fish, and even whales. When caribou were herded into water, hunters in their kayaks could make an easy kill. VanStone (1989) provided a full description of hunting techniques on Nunivak Island. The throwing of darts or light spears was often assisted by a throwing board or *atlatl* that extended the leverage of the throwing arm, making it possible to hit a wary seal from a considerable distance. In photograph 36 a variety of hunting tools can be seen on the kayaks' decks, along with the paddles. Bone or ivory supports are attached to the gunwales and pulled through the leather straps that cross the kayaks in three different places. The supports and straps kept the harpoons and paddles from falling into the water (see Fienup-Riordan 2005:71).

The man in the kayak third from the right has draped a gut parka over the edge of the cockpit. Gut parkas also appear in photographs 24 and 58. These watertight parkas fashioned from seal intestines were commonly worn by kayakers. According to Betty Kobayashi Issenman, humidity from the wearer's body could pass to the outside, but no water came inside (1997:74). Once the hood strings were pulled and the bottom secured and lashed over the rim of the cockpit, a wearer remained dry when paddling through waves or even after a capsize (see Adney and Chapelle 1964:227–229; Fienup-Riordan 2007).

No 34 Native Boat & St Michael Natives Alaska

Photograph No. 37. Native boat and St. Michael Natives, Alaska.

Umiaqs

The watercraft in photographs 37 and 38 are open skin boats, or umiaqs. Photograph 37 shows a man sitting high in the stern and six others at rest. The non-Native in the middle of the umiaq appears to be the same man standing fourth from the right in photograph 40, of the Stoney expedition. Photograph 38, taken at Port Clarence, is of a very large umiaq with at least seventeen paddlers and passengers. They appear to be transporting trade goods. Steam whaleships stopped in at Port Clarence to take advantage of coal and supplies brought there for the whaleships. Consequently, Natives traveled there to trade with the whaleships. The logbook of the *Bear* indicates that an umiaq was at Port Clarence from July 11 to 17. The vessels in the distance are the trading schooner *Clara Light* and the steamer *Alliance* (Bockstoce pers. comm., April 2005). Both *Alliance* and *Clara Light* were owned by James McKenna, among others. James McKenna was the master of the *Alliance*, and he was the agent for both the *Alliance* and the *Clara Light*. McKenna and several others had bought *Alliance* in 1885 as a tender for the whaling ships. The *Whalemen's Shipping List* of October 26, 1886, reported that *Clara Light* was lost in the Arctic Ocean at

Nº 38 Omiak or Family Canoe & Natives, Port Clarence, Alaska

Photograph No. 38. Umiak or family canoe and Natives, Port Clarence, Alaska.

some uncertain date (*Whalemen's Shipping List*). Bockstoce (2006:65) reported that she was abandoned in the ice fifteen miles north of Point Franklin, Alaska, sometime after September 3, 1886.

Kayaks were normally used only by men. Umiaqs, on the other hand, were used by both men and women. Women often rowed, while men paddled (Murdoch 1892:335). Rowers and paddlers sat on thwarts attached to stringers below the gunwales. Large umiaqs were guided by steersmen using a steering oar or a paddle. Kayaks were all-purpose hunting boats that could be stealthily paddled to get close to small prey. Umiaqs were useful for carrying heavier freight and Native families along the coast, up rivers, and to offshore islands (Adney and Chapelle 1964:182). Dog teams were hitched to the loaded umiaqs when going up river; while people sat in the umiaqs, the dog teams ran along the riverbanks. These versatile boats also served as shelters for travelers. When tipped up on one side, poles or paddles were used to support the boat on its gunwale. An example can be seen in photograph 53, where an umiaq on the left side of the photograph is propped up with some form of support.

These skin-covered boats also played a major role in hunting bowhead whales and walruses. Family members and communities were bound together by membership in whaling crews. Whaling captains usually had high status in the community. Like her husband, the whaling captain's wife was a prestigious figure in the community who had the responsibility of providing food to the crew and distributing whale meat and blubber to the people of the village. When a crew lacked the required numbers when going after walrus or seals, women who were not menstruating were allowed to fill in (Murdoch 1892:335).

With kayak construction, anthropometric measurements were essential. However, such measurements were not necessarily used by an umiaq builder, there being no need for a personal fit (Adney and Chapelle 1964:182). Umiaqs were covered with the skin of walrus, bearded seal (*ugruk*), or occasionally polar bear skin. The frameworks of umiaqs were different from their kayak cousins. Instead of a complicated internal skeleton with longitudinal stringers lashed to the frames, the skeleton of an umiaq resembled that of a wooden boat with the outer planking removed. John Murdoch (1892:335–344), Adney and Chapelle (1964:184–186), and VanStone (1989:17–20) provided descriptions of the construction technique. A wide timber extended from bow to stern along the internal length and acted as a keelson or the "backbone" of the boat. This timber gave the umiaq strength in place of a keel. Typically, the keelson was fashioned from a small tree, and the roots and branches were fashioned to become the stem and stern posts. Floors—short lengths of spruce, willow, fir or driftwood—were then lashed to that timber. The last stages of construction involved inserting the stringers and then lashing the frames to the floors and stringers. A hide covering was stretched to fit tightly over the skeleton. This covering was made of double-stitched skins sewn by women. It was then secured by more lashings to the gunwales. The covering was oiled and the seams well greased. During the winter the covering was removed and stored and the umiaq was placed high on a rack, safe from dogs.

Umiaqs had slightly flared bows to keep the paddler dry in frigid and choppy seas. They also had flat bottoms in order to land people and cargo on beaches where there were no wharves or jetties. As Murdoch (1892:335) suggests, in order to form a mind's-eye picture of an umiaq, imagine a fisherman's dory with its flared sides, flat bottom, and narrow bow and stern. Frequently there was a mortise cut in the keelson near the bow, in which a mast with a sail could be stepped, supported by stays and shrouds (Murdoch 1892:335). Early sails were made of woven grass, reindeer or caribou skin, or walrus or bearded seal intestine. The British Museum holds a 10 x 10 foot walrus-intestine sail from the Kotzebue area donated by British naval captain Frederick W. Beechey in 1828. Cloth sails were increasingly used in the later nineteenth century as trade goods appeared and as wrecked whaleships gave up their own sails. Umiaqs outfitted with masts can be seen in photograph 41 as the *Bear* takes on the members and equipment of Naval Lieutenant George Stoney's Northern Alaska Exploring Expedition.

Port Clarence

This is one of the photographs that presents a puzzle. Both this photograph from the McGoldrick Collection and an identical photograph from the Kennedy Collection at the New Bedford Whaling Museum (1982.40.40) have the same caption indicating that the photograph was taken at Port Clarence. However, another identical photograph in the Kennedy Collection (1979.26.74) and the same photograph in the Healy Collection (HL 20886) identify these people as "Natives of Sheshalik, Hotham Inlet – Alaska," which would mean that they were from an area northwest of Port Clarence, across the Seward Peninsula and near present-day Kotzebue, Alaska.

The group photographed here includes a woman wearing a cloth dress, probably gotten in trade, tight at the waist, and pulled over her other clothing. She appears to have a tattoo on her chin. Next to her are two men and a girl. In front are three children. The two men wear labrets, which were bone, stone, or ivory plugs inserted in the skin below the lip, sometimes worn on both sides of the mouth. The man on the left wears a small labret. The large white labret worn by the man to the right appears to be composed of a glass bead that is inserted into a substance such as ivory. It was not uncommon for the weight

Nº 39 Native Group at Port Clarence. Behring Seas.

Photograph No. 39. Native group at Port Clarence, Bering Sea.

of the labret to pull down the lower lip, as appears to be happening in this photograph. Fitzhugh et al. (1982:144-147), among others, suggest that men wore labrets in order to resemble walruses, a likeness that was enhanced by their clothes. The three parkas worn by the people standing in the back have white fur hanging on either side of the neck from the hood of the parka. Oakes and Riewe, drawing on the work of observers such as Murdoch (1892), and Nelson (1899), suggest that for the Northwest Coast of Alaska from Wales to Barrow:

> Triangular gussets of white or other contrasting skin were inserted into each
> side of the center front of most parkas. These usually served to anchor the
> hood to the body of the garment, and their tusk-like appearance was thought
> to imbue the wearer of the parka with the strength of the walrus (2007:43).

Also, elders were able to identify the origin of the parka through observing slight variations in the width and length of these gussets and geometric skin patterns (Oakes and Riewe 2007:55). Indeed, photograph 54, taken at Icy Cape northwest of Point Hope, shows parkas with a variety of widths of these white gussets. While there were regional differences, Edward Nelson commented on the similarity in patterns of parkas between Point Barrow and the mouth of the Yukon (in Ray 1981:52). Dorothy Jean Ray has described the ceremonial parkas worn in the north. These parkas were made of squirrel fur and had gores or insets of white reindeer skin. Also in the north, parkas were often made with hoods, while to the south, along the Kuskokwim and in the Interior, parkas went without them (Ray 1981:52). White caribou fur was rare, and domesticated reindeer skin from Chukchi herders was a much-desired trade item. Traders brought these furs across from Chukotka to the trade fairs on the shoreline of Alaska, such as at Sisualik near present-day Kotzebue (see discussion of photograph 43).

No 40 Lt Stoneys Camp at Hotham Inlet Kotzebue Sound

Photogrpah No. 40. Lt. Stoney's camp at Hotham Inlet, Kotzebue Sound.

Kotzebue Sound

The explorer Lt. Otto von Kotzebue named Kotzebue Sound after himself. This was done, Kotzebue wrote, in "compliance with the general wish of my companions" (Orth 1967; Ray 1975:62). The Russian Count Rumiantsev had financed Kotzebue's expedition to search for a northeast passage from the Pacific to the Atlantic. According to James VanStone (1977:75, n. 69), Kotzebue and his party were the first Europeans to enter the sound when they came in August 1816. In 1826 Captain Frederick W. Beechey named an inlet off the sound for Sir Henry Hotham, a lord of the British Admiralty (see Orth 1967).

Photographs 40 and 41 are of Naval Lt. George Stoney's exploring expedition. Lt. Stoney of the U.S. Navy and Lt. John Cantwell of the Revenue Marine were competitors in the exploration of the Kobuk River, at the time often called the Kowak or Putnam River. The river flows south and west from the Brooks Range and empties into Kotzebue Sound. It was considered to be a possible rescue route from the northern coast of Alaska for whaling crews whose ships were crushed in the ice. Such a route would provide access when the ice in the Chukchi and Arctic Seas prevented rescue parties from reaching the far north by sea.

Nº 41 Embarking Lt Stoneys Expedition at Cape Blossom

Photograph No. 41. Embarking Lt. Stoney's expedition at Cape Blossom.

Both Stoney and Cantwell explored the area in 1885. Lt. Stoney set up Camp Purcell in 1885 at Hotham Inlet on Kotzebue Sound. He used this camp, named in honor of an ensign who had been invalided back to San Francisco before the party's arrival in Kotzebue Sound the summer before, as a staging point for supplies that were ferried up the Kobuk River. On August 11, 1885, as Stoney was ascending the Kobuk River in the steam launch *Explorer,* Cantwell passed him going downriver (Cantwell in Healy 1887:46). Cantwell was then picked up by Michael Healy and the *Corwin* at Kotzebue Sound. Stoney went on to spend the winter up the Kobuk River at a camp he called Fort Cosmos, named after a favorite club in San Francisco frequented by his officers. Stoney and his men spent the winter exploring widely. Passed Assistant Engineer Abraham V. Zane had experience in the Arctic: he had served together with Stoney on the *Rodgers* in an expedition to find the *Jeannette,* lost to the ice north of Siberia. He travelled as far as St. Michael and back to Fort Cosmos, and Passed Assistant Surgeon Francis S. Nash, who had served on the *Alert* in the 1884 expedition to find Adolphus Greely's party in the eastern Arctic, was sent to an inland trading post for Yukon River Natives. He returned six days later with several of those Natives (Smith 1913:13; Stoney 1899:561).

The group of seventeen men and three dogs in photograph 40, captioned "Lt. Stoney's Camp at Hotham Inlet Kotzebue Sound," includes Taataruaq, or "grandfather" or "great uncle." He is the tall man standing sixth from the left. Taataruaq was the guide and interpreter who helped Lt. John Cantwell on his explorations into the interior of Alaska in 1884 and 1885. He also was part of the Stoney party pictured here. Taataruaq appears in photograph 44, captioned "Old Reliable." The man standing fourth from the right with his hand upraised is probably the white person in the umiaq in photograph 37.

On the reverse of this photograph, in different writing from the caption on the front, is written "Cape Smyth ^ Koon x Hamlet < J Fernandez." (Each one of these names is preceded by a symbol which can also be seen in the caption on the front of the photograph.) The symbols are written over the caption. Assuming the placement is correct, Koon (the "^" is visible in the caption in the "a" of "Hotham" Inlet) is standing seventh from the right. First Lt. Oscar Hamlet of the *Bear,* whose symbol "x" is in the "H" of "Hotham," is standing next to Koon, eighth from the right. J. Fernandez (the symbol "<" appears in the "N" of "No.") is the first fully visible man on the far left. William H. Koon was master/captain of the *Louisa,* a bark from San Francisco that struck ice in a gale on September 24, 1883, off Point Hope, Alaska (Bockstoce 2006:65). Earlier in his career, between 1876 and 1882, Koon had been master of the *Helen Mar.* He was master of the *Ocean* in 1885 but did not seem to have a command in 1886. It is not clear what he was doing in Hotham Inlet, unless he was involved in trading. The following year he was master of the *John P. West*, a bark out of New Bedford. J. Fernandez may have had an Azorean background, not unusual for members of whaling crews. In 1887, a John Fernandez was a seaman on the *Lagoda*, a whaling bark out of New Bedford (see National Maritime Digital Library). We suggest that the person to the far right, with his hand on a dog, strongly resembles the Francis S. Nash identified as No. 26 in a photo of the members of the Greely Relief Expedition (www.history.navy.mil/photos/images/h02000/h02875a.jpg). We also suggest that the man standing sixth from the right, who also has a dog that appears well acquainted with him, may be Passed Assistant Engineer Abraham V. Zane.

The Benham Collection information does not shed much light on this photograph, for the caption merely says "Group of Men by Ocean." The same photograph in the Kennedy Collection acquired in the 1979 bequest to the New Bedford Whaling Museum is titled "Camp of the N.A. Exploring Expedition, Hotham Inlet." The confusion as to the place where the photograph was taken (Cape Smyth, as it says on the reverse of the McGoldrick collection photo, or Hotham Inlet, as it says on the front of the same photo) could have arisen because Ensign William Howard of Stoney's party was picked up by the *Bear* at Cape Smyth, Barrow, Alaska, on Friday, August 13, after this photograph was taken. Howard had explored north from Stoney's camp, Fort Cosmos, and followed the Colville River, arriving in the Barrow area. Cape Smyth was the site of the signal station built by Lt. Patrick Henry Ray in 1881–1883 for the first International Polar Year investigation. The weathervane in this photograph may have resembled equipment that was visible at Ray's signal station. That station is depicted in photograph 56. Since Taataruaq was known to be from the Kotzebue area, and because he was Stoney and Cantwell's guide in the Kobuk River region, we can be reasonably sure that he was photographed in the region of Kotzebue Sound and not at Cape Smyth. The conflicting legends, front and back, as well as the lack of identification of other people standing on the shore, raise questions about when the captions for these photographs were written. Someone who knew a few of the men standing on the shore apparently added the information about three of the men after the fact.

Photograph 43, "Native Camp at Hotham Inlet Kotzebue Sound," shows tents lined up along a beach ridge that is probably at Sisualik, Hotham Inlet in Kotzebue Sound. The caption in the Healy Collection says it is the "Indian Summer Rendezvous at Sheshalik, Kotzebue Sound—Alaska." Sheshalik, or Sisualik,

Photograph No. 43. Native camp at Hotham Inlet, Kotzebue Sound.

Nu 44 Old Honesty. Tatarook. Native of Kotzebue

Photograph No. 44. Old Honesty. Tatarook, Native of Kotzebue Sound.

is at the northern end of the inlet. The name means "place where there are white whales," or beluga (Hooper 1884:39; Ray 1975:113). Beluga were most easily killed when they swam in shallow water near the shore, which they often did at Sisualik.

In the photograph there are at least twenty-one tents made of wood frames, placed in order on a beach ridge. In the foreground the tents are covered with caribou skins. Toward the back the tents are covered with cloth, and some have caribou-hide door flaps. These tents are tall and narrow, similar to the tent photographed at Cape Lisburne (photo 52) but different from the domed tent that appears in photograph 53, taken at Point Lay. One can just see some people sitting in the opening to the tent farthest to the right, and a man is standing behind the tent in a fur parka with two distinctive white tippets.

As noted in photograph 40, the *Bear* was in the area of Hotham Inlet between July 19 and 22, 1886. The logbook reported on visits to Lt. Stoney's camp and noted that Natives visited the *Bear* and the *Alliance* in Kotzebue Sound but said nothing about the Native camp. Native trade fairs occurred throughout coastal Alaska and were an important means of exchanging goods and information and for maintaining individual trade relationships with trusted trading partners from widely dispersed villages. Among other goods, people from the interior of Alaska brought furs such as wolverine and wolf to exchange for marine mammals and fish. Siberians were known to attend fairs in Alaska, bringing reindeer hides with them in exchange for natural resources they did not have. At Sisualik, people came from as far north as Point Hope, from as far south as Cape Prince of Wales, from the Diomede Islands, and from the Chukotka Peninsula (Hooper 1884:39; see also Burch 2005:180–189). According to Hooper, captain of the *Corwin* during its 1881 summer cruise, that year at Sisualik there were two hundred tents made of cotton drill set in orderly rows, with kayaks, overturned umiaqs, and sleds and dogs. Edward Nelson was on the same cruise, and he photographed the scene. He described the "almost military precision" of the encampment. The tents extended more than a mile along the shoreline, providing housing for between 600 and 800 people. Nelson said the tents were covered with untanned winter caribou skins, hair side out. Some of the tents were then covered with drill or calico similar in style to the coverings seen in this photograph (1899:260–262).

John Murdoch (1892:84) described similar summer tents in the Point Barrow region. They were made by lashing five or six twelve-foot poles together. The tent at the base was about twelve feet in diameter. A bentwood tent hoop was placed six feet above ground, with poles (sometimes umiaq oars or spears) lashed across the hoop. Murdoch describes canvas (sailcloth from wrecked whaling ships or drill) covering the frame in a spiral fashion, beginning at the top. According to Cantwell's report in 1884 (Healy 1889:81) and Lee and Reinhardt (2003:94), smoke holes were not needed for cooking because people cooked outside in the summer.

In late August 1884, Michael Healy, by then captain of the *Corwin*, left a note for Lt. Cantwell asking him to find out when the gathering at Hotham Inlet occurred and how many attended. On August 21, 1884, Cantwell counted six hundred people at the gathering and added that many had already left (Cantwell in Healy 1889:71). However, the encampment may already have been moved to Kotzebue in 1884, for Cantwell reports that he moved his own camp

> to a sand spit projecting into Kotzebue Sound, from the southern side of the
> entrance to Hotham Inlet, where the coast natives of the several settlements
> from Bering Strait, northward to Cape Lisburne, had rendezvoused to trade
> with the natives of the interior living on the Nöitoc, Kowak, and Selawick
> Rivers (Cantwell in Healy 1889:77).

The following year Captain Healy, in his *Report of the Cruise of the Revenue Marine Steamer* Corwin, *1885,* reported that no Natives had arrived at Sisualik by July 1 for trade, and Lt. Cantwell had trouble finding a boat for traveling up the Kowak River. However, Healy wrote that on August 4, 1885, there were about a thousand Natives from inland and along the shore at Hotham Inlet fishing, drying salmon, and trading. When the *Corwin* returned at the end of August, there were only a few people remaining, as the Natives had returned home (Healy 1887:13).

There is some question as to whether the Native rendezvous in 1886 was still being held at Sisualik or had relocated to Kotzebue. John Bockstoce drew on Nelson (1899:231) and Burch (1998:215) to argue that

> About the year 1885 the natives moved the site of their trade rendezvous in
> Kotzebue Sound from Sheshalik to *Qikiqtagruk,* the location of the present
> town of Kotzebue, most probably because the trading vessels could approach
> closer to shore there (Bockstoce 2009:336).

Burch noted that the increasing dependence of Natives on American trade goods led

> ...apparently in 1884, to a shift in the location of the fair from Sisualik to the "Kotzebue peninsula," an appendage of Baldwin Peninsula on which the city of Kotzebue now stands (2005:187).

This photograph may well be of a Native fishing or hunting camp and not of the larger trade rendezvous. The fact that people were drying meat on the racks indicates not so much a trading event but instead the procurement of dried meat for the winter. The meat may have been fish, beluga, or bearded seal, although mid-July may be late in the season for bearded seal (Burch, pers. comm., January 9, 2010).

In photograph 44 Tatarook, or Taataruaq, stands in front of a conical cloth tent similar to those in photograph 43. The sleds, or sledges, in this photograph were used for pulling heavy loads and were more sturdy than the sled at Indian Point, shown in photograph 20. Taataruaq is wearing a cotton pullover, leather pants, and boots. He also appears in photograph 40. There he is the sixth person from the left, wearing a fur parka. A copy of photograph 44 appears in Healy's 1884 report of the cruise of the *Corwin* (Healy 1889, opposite p. 86), and an etching of Taataruaq appears in Healy's report of the 1885 cruise of the *Corwin* (1887, opposite p. 53). Lt. Cantwell explored the Kobuk River in 1884 and 1885. In 1884, Healy sent Taataruaq as a guide and interpreter for Cantwell. Cantwell was trying to determine the location of the real mouth of the Kobuk River and had wandered for two days before Taataruaq caught up with him and showed him the way (Strobridge and Noble 1999:84). Taataruaq accompanied Cantwell again in 1885. Cantwell was impressed at Taataruaq's skill at ensuring the Natives would work for them—often as long as fourteen hours a day. Cantwell relied heavily on him and commented frequently on his quick-minded intelligence (Cantwell in Healy 1887:33).

From the Logbook

On July 19, 1886, the *Bear* arrived at Kotzebue Sound to meet Stoney's party and to bring them mail. In the logbook of the *Bear* for July 19, Lt. Benham noted:

> 9.45 came to off Hotham Inlet in 4 fs veering 15 f to starb. Anchor the spit bearing N.E 1/3 N Cape Krusenstern W and 1/2 W. Sent in boat with 1st Lieut to communicate with the Stoney party. End of watch cloudy and squally with strong S E winds. The ice drifting rapidly to the Northward.

The following day, July 20, Lt. Benham wrote that the *Bear*

> Steamed around the shoal off Cape Blossom. 4 to 6 PM squalls and rough sea. 4.20 came to in 4 fms veering 20 fms to starbd. Anchor C. Blossom. . . . Hoisted out steam launch and sent her under charge of lst Lieut Hamlet to communicate with Lieut. Stoney's party in Hotham Inlet.

Since Lt. Kennedy made no entries in the logbook when Hamlet was visiting Stoney's party for the second time, he may have accompanied Lt. Hamlet back to Stoney's party. His photograph of the Stoney expedition would have been taken at this time. Lt. Stoney was away between July 16 and 24, surveying the Selawik River and Selawik Lake. Passed Assistant Engineer Abraham V. Zane was in charge of Camp Purcell, and on Thursday, July 22, Zane paid an official visit to the *Bear*. Then she made her way north toward Point Hope and Point Barrow, leaving the Stoney party until her return south a month later. On August 23 the *Bear* rounded Cape Krusenstern and hauled up for Cape Blossom, anchoring in four fathoms, or about twenty-four feet, of water. In the latter part of the noon to 4 PM watch there was an increasing gale accompanied with snow squalls. Dunwoody noted that they found Lt. Stoney's party encamped near the cape, but the sea was too rough to go inshore. The following day, with a smooth sea, six members of Stoney's party visited the vessel, and the crew was employed receiving and stowing supplies from the expedition. Photograph 41 depicts this embarkation. On August 25 Stoney and his party came on board

> …with all their effects and ten men for passage to San Francisco and also the Two native families (2 men 3 women and two children) of the expedition with two Omiaks for passage to St. Michaels. The steamer "Explorer" was turned over to this vessel for transportation to St. Michaels. The crew employed in stripping her of all movable work—Pilot house, smokestack, and Paddle Wheel, etc. + stowing them on board.

That afternoon they hoisted aboard and dismantled Stoney's steam cutter, the *Helena,* which is visible on the right side of the *Bear.* The *Bear* got underway at 4:45 AM on August 26, with the flat-bottomed *Explorer* in tow, shaping a course south toward Norton Sound and St. Michael.

Nº 45 Crew of the Bear watering ship at Cape Thompson

Photograph No. 45. Crew of the *Bear* watering ship at Cape Thompson.

Point Hope

On August 2, 1826, British Navy Captain Frederick W. Beechey and his ship the *Blossom* "closed with a high cape" overlooking the Chukchi Sea "which I named after Mr. Deas Thomson, one of the commissioners of the navy" (Beechey 1832, 1:359). Beechey and his crew chose this height of land for a signal post for John Franklin, who in 1825–1826 explored the Mackenzie River to the Beaufort Sea and then traveled west in anticipation of meeting Beechey. Captain Beechey wrote:

> As this was a fit place to erect a signal-post for Captain Franklin, we landed and were met upon the beach by some Esquimaux, who eagerly sought an exchange of goods. Very few of their tribe understood better how to drive a bargain than these people, and it was not until they had sold almost all they could spare, that we had any peace (Beechey 1832, 1:359).

His party climbed the cape and saw off to the north and west a long spit of land

> as far as the eye could reach. As this point had never been placed on our charts, I named it Point Hope, in compliment to Sir William Johnstone Hope (Beechey 1832, 1:362–363).

At the time of Beechey's voyage, Hope, who had a long career in the British navy, was a lord of the British Admiralty.

Cape Thompson was important as an aid to navigation and as a source of fresh water. In 1900, Lt. David H. Jarvis wrote about this cape in the *Alaska Coast Pilot*. Jarvis had served on the *Bear* and in 1897 was in charge of the winter rescue operation that brought reindeer from the coast of Alaska up to Point Barrow to provide food for whalemen whose ships had been caught in the ice. In the *Coast Pilot*, Jarvis recommended looking for fresh water near highlands such as Cape Thompson. Five headlands form the cape, and Jarvis wrote that the center point should be determined, and

> [I]n the ravine south of this point there is a small stream, from which good water can easily be obtained. Directly off the watering place anchorage may be had in 5 fathoms, sandy bottom (Jarvis 1900:55).

In photograph 45, five seamen stand on shore with buckets. They are taking fresh water out of a creek that flows into the Chukchi Sea. This stream is presumably the one recommended by Lt. Jarvis. The *Bear*'s boat is drawn up on the beach, and the *Bear* is anchored

No 46 Chief at Point Hope "Old Unreliable"

Photograph No. 46. Chief at Point Hope, "Old Unreliable."

offshore. Chunks of drift ice can be seen floating by. The photograph was probably taken on Sunday, July 25, for Lt. Benham wrote that from 4 to 8 AM on that day the crew "watered ship at Cape Thompson." From 8 AM until noon the crew continued to water the ship and also cleaned her water tanks. By 3:45 PM, twelve hours after they had started, they finished watering, having taken on board 1,530 gallons. From 4 to 6 PM there was heavy ice drifting to the north and west and the boats were hoisted onto the *Bear*.

Photograph 46 of the "Chief at Point Hope," or "Old Unreliable," was taken of the person identified by John Bockstoce as "a man of exceptional size, strength, cunning, and gall" (1986:199). He is labeled in the caption as "Old Unreliable" in contrast to the supposedly more reliable Taataruaq, "Old Honesty," shown in photograph 44. This man, Ataŋauraq, is standing on the deck of the *Bear* with his back to a gangway, in the same place where the photograph of Lt. Benham was taken. The shoreline is in the distance. His clothes are a combination of Native and European styles. He is wearing a fur jacket with what appear to be ivory buttons as well as mattress-ticking trousers and a cap similar to those worn by some of the white men in other photos in this collection. He also has two labrets, one large and one small. The distinctive labret on the left is similar to some from Point Hope described by Nelson. Those labrets were made of white quartz, about an inch and a half in diameter, with half a blue bead attached to the surface (Nelson 1899:48). Walrus ivory may also have formed the base for the large labret. His short summer hunting boots rise to just above the ankle. The soles of the boots are probably made of bearded seal skin. The skin forming the soles was carefully crimped and sewn in a fashion still characteristic of the northern Alaska style of boot making.

Ataŋauraq and Captain Healy knew each other well. Lowenstein (2008) has written of Native testimony to the fact that they traded and drank with each other. There are two other known photographs of Ataŋauraq. That he was photographed at least three times attests to the power he exercised and the white men's interest in him. One of the two other photos, taken on the deck of the *Corwin* in 1881, is part of the Edward W. Nelson Collection at the Smithsonian's National Anthropological Archives. In it, Ataŋauraq appears together with four other Native men. His distinctive labrets identify him, for he is wearing the large white oblong labret with the attached glass bead on the right side of his lip (Burch 1981:18), which he also wears in the photograph here. The other photograph, in the Sheldon Jackson Collection, Presbyterian Historical Society, was apparently taken in 1887 (Burch 1981:16). In that photograph he is wearing the same labrets and stands with one of his five wives outside one of the buildings of the whaling station at

Jabbertown, down the coast from his own village. His parka is of white and brown Siberian reindeer skin, and his wife's is made of cloth (Burch 1981:16). She wears leather pants and has on low summer boots. He has on leather breeches that come just below his knee, apparently over leather pants. He also wears low summer boots.

Ataŋauraq was a Native middleman who controlled the trade between whalemen and Natives in the Point Hope area. He was also a whaleboat captain (*umialik*) and a shaman at the same time that he was a tyrant and a murderer. Charles Brower, who had been on the *Grampus* when it was caught in the ice off Indian Point in May and June 1886, first met Ataŋauraq in 1884. Brower had come north with the Pacific Steam Whaling Company to help manage the coal veins at the Corwin Coal Mine near Cape Lisburne, north of Point Hope. Brower wrote vivid accounts of his encounters with Ataŋauraq and of his time spent whaling while staying in Point Hope (Brower mss., also 1947).

According to John Kelly and later John Bockstoce, Ataŋauraq knew of Quwaaren, or Goharren, the trader from Indian Point described earlier, and wanted to be equally as powerful (Bockstoce 1986:199; Kelly et al. 1890:9–11). The whalemen, traders, and the Revenue Marine often sought out Native men at villages along the coast with whom they could establish trade relationships. Some of the more aggressive among them, like Ataŋauraq, were happy to take on this role. The word "chief" was a misnomer, because Ataŋauraq and other men like him were technically not chiefs in the sense of hereditary and aristocratic leadership typical of chiefdoms. The term *umialik* was often used, as this referred to someone who not only owned and was captain of a whaleboat but also was responsible for the welfare of those who went whaling with him.

Whalemen sought to set up a whaling station at Point Hope, but Ataŋauraq, the local strong man, made them stay about six miles from Point Hope in an area that became known as Jabbertown (see Bockstoce 2009:346). The origin of the name has been debated, though it may have arisen because of the many different languages spoken by the whalemen (Lowenstein 2008:91–92). Although Ataŋauraq had at least five wives, he angered men in the community because of his abusive relationships with still more women. He was reported by John Kelly to have killed five men and one woman. Kelly wrote that "in his efforts to become absolute master of his people he passed from tyranny to assassination" (Kelly et al. 1890:11). Charles Brower made reference to Ataŋauraq's "private graveyard" in which four bodies were

No 47 Chiefs House at Point Hope

Photograph No. 47. Chief's house at Point Hope.

preserved on a single rack above the ground (1947:89). A number of Point Hopers moved away because of his increasingly intimidating and unpredictable behavior. As Kelly said,

> He inspired such terror that every year people left for distant hunting-grounds, till it seemed that a few more years of his reign would have seen Tigara depopulated (Kelly et al. 1890:11).

After years of abuse from him, members of the community had had enough. He was killed on February 14, 1889, three years after this photograph was taken (see Rainey 1947:243). His death that night was reported in several ways. It has been said that his head was sliced off by the northern lights. Brower said that Ataŋauraq was shot through an open window above where he was sleeping and finished off by the sharp knife of a disgruntled wife (1947:149–150). Lowenstein (2008:139–143) refers to eyewitnesses in Point Hope at the time who told Froelich Rainey that two brothers, in revenge for an earlier murder in which Ataŋauraq was an accomplice, returned to Point Hope to kill him. One stood guard over the gut window of Ataŋauraq's house while the other crept in to shoot Ataŋauraq in the head as he lay sleeping between two wives. Unfortunately, we know little of what Michael Healy thought about the death of his trading partner, for those records have been lost. Lowenstein does report that when Healy arrived that summer on the *Bear* he pursued one of Ataŋauraq's killers to Cape Lisburne but did not apprehend him (2008:143–144).

Photograph 47 is most likely the house of Ataŋauraq. In August 1885, the *Corwin*, with Michael Healy as captain, put in at Point Hope to find the village temporarily deserted. The inhabitants had gone hunting or fishing. Three members of a whaling crew being taken south on the *Corwin* stole goods from some of the houses, and Captain Healy placed them in irons (Healy 1887:12). The winter of 1885–1886 had been a devastating one for the people of Point Hope. Dozens of people died. Walrus and whale had already been scarce, the caribou herds had declined or moved away, and the result was famine. That winter "many dogs were eaten, and in some instances the walrus-hide coverings to canoes were cut up and made into soup" (Aldrich 1889:35; Burch 1981:17).

The village of Point Hope, also known as Tiqiġaq, is located on a long spit of gravel and sand formed by sediments from the Kukpuk River and the wave action of the Chukchi Sea. Point Hope has been continuously occupied for at least 2,500 years (Foote 1992; Rainey 1947; VanStone 1962). Its location at the

N.º 49 Native House at Point Hope

Photograph No. 49. Native house at Point Hope.

Nu 48 Natives at Point Hope. Arctic Ocean

Photograph No. 48. Natives at Point Hope, Arctic Ocean.

end of the spit has made it an ideal place for hunting marine mammals. This *tiqiġaq* or "index finger" juts into the Chukchi Sea and provides access to migrating bowhead and beluga whales as well as to bearded seals and walruses. Semisubterranean houses of several cultural traditions have been found there (see, for example, Giddings and Anderson 1986; Larsen and Rainey 1948). These dwellings were dug into the beach ridges. They were supported by whale bone and wood, and sod and moss were placed above and around the houses, acting as insulation from the weather.

Whale bone uprights formed an entrance to the main living area. The entrance was often south-facing for sun and warmth. The entrance led down and through a tunnel, which had antechambers to the side for cooking, storage, and sometimes for sleeping. From the entranceway a circular hole allowed for access into the living area. Floors of smoothed, split wood were laid, and wood and whale bone helped create walls. A sleeping platform was raised enough to provide storage space or additional bedding for guests (Lee and Reinhardt 2003:78). Heat and some light were created by burning moss wicks in seal-oil lamps. The long entranceway helped ensure that the cold was left outside, and white visitors often remarked on the heat and closeness of the area inside.

The rack above this house was made with whale bone and driftwood. The intent was to keep goods out of the way of dogs and other predators. Sleds and umiaqs would often be placed above ground, as would skins, furs, walrus skin rope, and inflated seal floats. Here, however, an umiaq is lying on its side at the right of the image. The photograph shows a sledge, a barrel, and a gut window. There is a chimney just behind the window. It appears that a bent-wood tent hoop rests against a support at the rear in the center of the photograph, just behind and to the right of the gut window. That hoop may have been part of the support structure for a summer tent (see Lee and Reinhardt 2003:94–96). There is a skin bag hanging from a whale rib, and two containers are on the ground near the sled. Such containers were made of bent wood or baleen and were used to hold water, food, entrails, or urine. A sketch apparently based on this photograph appears in Sheldon Jackson's report on education in Alaska (Jackson 1894:941). The details are very similar, with the addition of a person's head appearing in the gap in the stones lying between the two containers, indicating the entrance into the house. Other houses are visible in the distance, again with whale bone supports. Masks were displayed not only in ceremonial houses but also in houses, in house tunnel entrances, and in graveyards (Ray 1967). In this photograph there may be a mask hanging off the right pole of the rack.

No 58 The oldest Known inhabitant on the Arctic Shores.

Photograph No. 58. Oldest known inhabitant on the arctic shores.

The houses were often rectangular, measuring twelve to fourteen feet long, eight to ten feet wide, and five to seven feet high (Lee and Reinhardt 2003:78) or even higher: Charles Brower reported that upon being given a challenge to wrestle someone up in Icy Cape, Ataŋauraq leapt into the air and kicked the gut window eight feet above the floor with both feet (Brower 1947:114). He was a man of imposing size, and his house may have had a higher ceiling than usual, but the houses could hold substantial numbers of people. Some houses were joined together, creating large family compounds of married brothers or cousins.

Photograph 49 is another view of a house, in profile. The house also has a rack with goods elevated high above the house, sledges, and whale bone. There are inflated sealskin floats hanging from the rack. The lower jaw of a walrus is fastened to the pole on the left front side of the rack (Lee and Reinhardt 2003:77; Murdoch 1892:75). These mandibles were used for support for crosspieces. A hoop leans against the house, just between the two large supports for the rack.

A photo taken in Point Hope in 1913 by W. B. Van Valin shows at least twenty-three houses like this side by side along the beach ridges, row by row, with an interval of thirty or forty feet between the rows (Kaplan and Barsness 1986:114–116). Much of the area in which these photographs were taken has since eroded into the sea, necessitating the movement of present-day Point Hope further along the peninsula, where prefabricated houses, brought in by barge and aircraft, have been placed in orderly rows.

In photograph 48, "Natives at Point Hope. Arctic Ocean," twenty-two people of all ages wear a variety of clothing styles in this carefully posed photograph. Some are amused, some less so. Several of the faces show close family connections. A very old man can be seen in the back row, fourth from the left, dressed in a seal gutskin parka. A hood covers his head. He is wearing a thin parka over the gutskin. Fienup-Riordan (2007:155) describes this practice as a means of staying especially warm. A woman in the middle is wearing a cloth covering over her head. The children in front are wearing a variety of boot styles: summer boots to the ankles and winter boots to the knees. The parkas also vary widely, and one man to the right appears to have a blanket or cape over his shoulders. Two men to the left of him are laughing down at a child, who appears equally engaged with the two men. To the far left, two men and a woman are wearing parkas with white tusk-like inserts, as are a man in the middle and two children on the far right.

This photograph was most likely not taken at Point Hope, even though the numbering sequence here and in the Kennedy Collection places the photograph in the series taken at Point Hope. An individual photograph (58) of the very old man who appears here, fourth from the left in the rear, is in this collection, titled "The Oldest Know [*sic*] Inhabitant on the Arctic Shores." The same photograph, of which there are two copies in the Healy Collection, was titled "Kowak River Native" (HL 20915). On the reverse of one of those copies there is an inscription that reads, "This old man put his head in the instrument and Lieut. Kennedy pulled the string quickly and here is the result." Yet another image offered for sale by an antiquarian bookseller, Aquila Books (2013), identified him as a "Kobuk River Eskimo Seen at Hotham Inlet, Alaska." This would place him in the Kotzebue Sound area. Furthermore, photograph 48 is labeled in the Healy Collection as "Natives at Sheshalik—Kotzebue Sound—Alaska." The old man's appearance also may indicate that he came from an area well to the south of Point Hope or more likely the interior, for instance the upper Noatak River or the lower Kobuk River (Burch pers. comm., January 8, 2010).

In 1826, Captain Beechey was struck by the "forest of stakes" that he could see on the long spit of land at Point Hope. In a 1904 letter E. J. Knapp wrote that this "weird Eskimo graveyard two miles and more in length resembled trunks of blasted trees…the bodies…dissolved" (Knapp 1904 in Lowenstein 2008:310). The graves, some of which appear in photograph 50, "Native Grave Yard at Point Hope," represented thousands of burials over time. Not all the dead were placed on platforms, but many were. In this photo a body is still intact; the legs of the deceased are visible and the knees are bent. What appear to be two sled runners stand upright on the left of the image (Bockstoce pers. comm., January 19, 2010). Skulls lie scattered on the ground below the bier.

Charles Brower wrote that the uprights were all mandibles of whales, set vertically in the ground. Some were small jawbones, not over ten feet long. To these jawbones were lashed the lower jaw of a walrus. Wood planks were laid on the walrus jawbones to create a platform similar to the racks above the houses in photographs 47 and 49. Brower (mss; 1947) noticed bodies on the ground, dragged there on an old sled that might have belonged to the deceased or someone in their family. The bodies were wrapped in old sleeping skins. Personal objects were left at the grave, often deliberately broken so no one would use them. He reported that the graveyard extended up toward the base of the point, looking like a forest of small trees. In the early twentieth century Augustus Hoare, missionary in Point Hope, enlisted "every living person of working age on the Point" (Lowenstein 2008:311) to remove the platforms and to bury the remains, many of them in mass graves. However, the graves of several shamans, including that of Ataŋauraq, can still be located (Lowenstein 2008:306, 308).

Na 50 Grave Yard @ Point Hope.

Photograph No. 50. Graveyard at Point Hope.

From the Logbook

The *Bear* spent from mid-morning on July 26 to 4 AM on July 27 at Point Hope. The weather was overcast and rainy. While there the crew washed their clothes. Lt. Benham reported "Crew washing clothes better part of watch." With heavy ice drifting down on the *Bear*, they "got underway and shifted anchorage."

On the *Bear*'s return journey, on the way home to San Francisco, she stopped in again from 5:50 PM on August 21 to August 22 at 4 PM, when it rained much of the time. During this return visit Lt. Benham confined Seaman W. Davis to single irons for insolence to the boatswain. Davis stayed in irons for twelve hours. No mention was made in the logbook of Ataŋauraq, of the houses, or of the graveyard. Yet Kennedy spent enough time on shore to photograph the house of Ataŋauraq, one other house, and the extensive Point Hope graveyard.

Cape Lisburne

> On August 21, 1778, Captain James Cook decided to look for a harbor, having turned back because of ice to the northeast at what he named Icy Cape. At this time the coast extended from S.W. to E., the nearest part four or five leagues distant. The southern extreme seemed to form a point, which was named Cape Lisburne (Cook 1842, 2:336).

Wilmot Vaughan, 4th Viscount Lisburne, was a lord commissioner of the admiralty from 1770 to 1782 (see Orth 1970 for a discussion of Cape Lisburne). Some people from Point Hope would move overland or by umiaq the forty miles north to Cape Lisburne to gather eggs on the highlands and to hunt for caribou in the summer. They returned to the cape to hunt for polar bear and seal in the winter.

In 1838 while at this cape the Russian explorer A. P. Kashevarov met twenty people from Point Hope, with two children and two umiaqs. Shortly after this encounter they noticed a tent occupied by seven people. The twelve-foot-high tent was made of caribou skins that were "wrapped around crossbars with the hair side out" (VanStone 1977:20). The tent Kashevarov described may have been similar to the one close to the beach seen in photograph 52.

N⁰ 52 Landing Place at Cape Lisbourn, Artic Ocean

Photograph No. 52. Landing place at Cape Lisburne, Arctic Ocean.

From the Logbook

At 5:05 AM on Tuesday, July 27, the *Bear* rounded Point Hope in moderate wind and fog. Lt. Kennedy noted that they steered northwest through drift ice, then at 6 AM set a course for Cape Lisburne. By 11 AM, still steaming through drift ice, the *Bear* hauled around Cape Lisburne. Early that afternoon a boat was sent in to "communicate with the shore Pacific Steam Whaling Station," where photograph 52 was taken. According to the logbook, this station had been recently abandoned. The building has vertical log sides and a log roof and at least three chimneys. A weathervane appears be mounted on the roof. About seven men are seated outside the building. To the left on the beach is a conical tent. To the right there are outbuildings, a dog, and several barrels.

While at Cape Lisburne, medical aid was rendered to a crew member of the whaling bark *Francis Palmer*, J. J. Haviside, master. On July 28, the officers visited several whaleships, both sail and steam. The latter were taking on coal at the Corwin Coal Mine, while the sailing whaleships may have stayed with the steam whaling fleet because of the ice that lay ahead. Photograph 11 shows *Belvedere* offshore of the coal seam, together with four other vessels. Lt. Kennedy noted that officers of the *Bear* boarded and examined six barks, including *Francis Palmer, Abraham Barker, Helen Mar, Reindeer, Mars,* and *Ocean,* as well as two steam whaleships, the *Belvedere* and the *Lucretia.*

This was a busy day, for the logbook reported that Emile Adams, formerly of the sunken bark *John Carver,* was taken on board from the bark *Ohio* until he could secure employment. Several hours later he found a position on the bark *Ocean.* Also, the *Bear* received three boxes of specimens for the Smithsonian Institution from the Pacific Steam Whaling Station at Cape Lisburne. Early in the evening, Lt. Dunwoody wrote:

> Received on board from station recently abandoned by Pacific Steam Whaling
> Co. Joe, his wife and two children destitute as passengers for St. Michaels
> they being unable to procure passage there and being destitute without food
> here and the means for obtaining the same.

The *Bear* left the coaling station on Friday, July 30, under steam, "carefully scanning the shoreline" for ice.

53 View at Point Lay Arctic Ocean.

Photograph No. 53. View at Point Lay, Arctic Ocean.

Point Lay

Point Lay is to the northeast of Point Hope and east of Cape Lisburne. Captain Frederick W. Beechey named it for the naturalist on board the *Blossom*, George Tradescant Lay (VanStone 1977:69, n. 16). In 1838, Kasheverov did not report any Natives living there. In 1881 to 1883, Patrick Henry Ray of the U.S. Army Signal Station at Barrow did not find many people there either, although the Natives may have been at one of the trade fairs at Sisualik or Icy Cape (Bockstoce pers. comm., 2012).

The *Bear* stopped at Point Lay on July 30 and 31. The image in the McGoldrick Collection was the most faded, but a digital enhancement brought out some very interesting features. A family is camped on the shoreline. To the left there is an umiaq propped on a gunwale, providing shelter from the wind. A portion of what appears to be a tent is in front of the umiaq, and just in front of that is another umiaq. Four people sit between the umiaq and the tent. The domed tent is made of skin, perhaps caribou. In front of the tent are a woman and a child holding a bow and arrow. Behind the tent are poles bearing stylized figures. The one on the left is a person with outstretched arms and a sun or moon or a drum. The other is a rectangle and an indeterminate object (see Lee and Reinhardt 2003:151, for a similar image). Dorothy Jean

Ray has written that poles with bird and animal carvings that represented protective spirits were found at summer camps in northern Alaska (Ray 1981:37). These sticks were not unlike memorial poles, which would be placed either at graves or by men's houses as part of a memorial feast that honored the dead (see Nelson 1899:363–379; Zagoskin 1967:122–123).

Charles Brower arrived at Point Lay in July 1886 on the *Grampus*, about the time this photograph was taken. According to Brower, a Siberian Native on board the *Grampus* refused to go on shore. He explained that, several years before, a group from Point Lay had been blown ashore on Siberia. The Point Lay men were killed and the women were taken as wives by the Siberians. He feared retribution (Brower 1947:79; see also Nelson 1899:330). As Burch (2005:29–30) made clear, such behavior had occurred all along the Alaska coastline.

John W. Kelly commented on the small number of households at Point Lay. His *Ethnographical Memoranda* (Kelly et al. 1890:18) recorded "tribes dying out." Only three huts were left there, he wrote. This may have been due to the spread of disease and to the collapse of the caribou population, events noted in Point Hope and elsewhere in Northwest Alaska at the time (see Burch 2012).

From the Logbook

At 3:45 PM on July 30 they anchored, and Lt. Dunwoody reported, "Natives from Pt Lay visiting the vessel." The following day Dunwoody noted "thick rainy weather" and that, because of the ice, they hauled anchor and moved to Icy Cape, coming to in six fathoms of water.

Icy Cape

Icy Cape was named by Captain James Cook, who turned back from his planned voyage to the east because of the formidable sea ice still present on August 15, 1778. He wrote, "The eastern extreme forms a point which was much encumbered with ice; for which reason it obtained the name Icy Cape" (1842, 2:334). The Native name for Icy Cape was Utuqqaq, "something old" (Lawrence Kaplan pers. comm., January 14, 2010). It was, in precontact time, a very large northwest coast settlement (VanStone 1977:70, n. 23, 24). Frederick W. Beechey described a village here in 1826. In 1838, Kashevarov and his party put into a lagoon from the sea on the north side of Icy Cape and found a "sizable village" of about three hundred people, identical in appearance to the people from Point Hope they had encountered at Cape Lisburne (VanStone 1977:26).

This remarkable trade gathering at Icy Cape includes seventeen children seated in the front row, twenty-one people in the second row, and twenty-six people standing. There are sixty-four people in all, and three sleepy dogs. Kennedy had in front of him the largest gathering documented in this set of photographs. The clothing is diverse, as might be expected of a group of people who have come from different areas. Many are dressed in what may have been their best clothing. Some, especially the men standing

No. 54. Native gathering at the trading house at Icy Cape.

in the rear, are wearing the distinctive parkas with white triangular tippets, or gussets, that are seen in photographs 39 and 48 and described by Oakes and Riewe (2007:43). The white tippets vary in size. The man standing third from the left in the back has wide tips, while the person standing fifth from the left has these tips connected to a white hood.

Three people, including a woman in the second row and two children, are wearing white parkas with white hoods. One person standing in the back and almost under the triangular portion of the roof of the trading and dance house is wearing a cape that is tied around the neck. Most of the men appear to wear labrets. The man standing sixth from the left has a pair of snow goggles hanging around his neck. The man who is fifth from the right (bending down to talk with someone kneeling in the second row) is wearing a headband.

Photograph 55 shows the structure that is visible behind the group in photograph 54. In this photograph the group has dispersed, although three people are standing under the dance house, and a bundle with contents that cannot be identified hangs on the right. There are hides hanging from the other side of the dance house, which appears to face the water.

The structure appears to be somewhat improvised and less permanently built than the descriptions of other such buildings indicate was the norm. The trading and dance house seen here appeared in Nelson's 1881 photograph of "Innuit at Icy Cape," which was printed in Hooper's report of the cruise of the *Corwin* (Hooper 1884:37). Many villages had ceremonial houses such as those described in the discussion of photograph 30. The Yup'ik had men's ceremonial houses. To the north these structures served as community centers, trading halls, and dance halls. Religious ceremonies were held there, and stories were told. Men often worked on equipment and trade goods inside and outside of the structures throughout the day (Murdoch 1892:80). They also served as schools for children (see Lee and Reinhardt 2003:108–110). Point Hope is reported to have had at least seven of these structures during the nineteenth century (Rainey 1947:244; see Lee and Reinhardt 2003:112). John Murdoch (1892:80) wrote that Lt. Patrick Henry Ray reported seeing one structure in northern Alaska that was 16 by 20 feet and 7 feet high.

Lee and Reinhardt estimate that the Icy Cape *qargi*'s span

> was at least seven by thirty feet and its pitched roof was about seven feet high in the middle. Skins or cloth covered both end walls and the rafters but left the side walls mostly exposed. At about the same time, a temporary *qarqi* [the same structure?] was said to have eighty caribou skins invested in its "tent cover" (Lantis 1947:105n134 in Lee and Reinhardt 2003:110).

From the Logbook

These two photographs were probably taken at the beginning of August. The *Bear* put in at Icy Cape on August 1. That day there was a heavy snow storm. Lt. Kennedy reported boarding and examining the whaling bark *Arnolda* of New Bedford, Marvin, master, and "rendered medical assistance to one of her crew." The *Bear* lay at anchor through August 2 to 10, cleaning, painting, whitewashing lockers, and fitting swinging boom pendants. The *Lucretia* came in to anchor on the fifth and on the sixth the *San Jose* came in to join them. By the seventh the *Arnolda* and the *Wanderer* had anchored as well. Heavy ice drifted to the south. Because of the weather and the ice, the *Bear* stayed anchored for nine days. There was plenty of time to perform the "usual morning duties," which were followed by more cleaning and whitewashing. Then the crew cleaned and washed the steerage and scraped and oiled the masts and spars. Finally, on the afternoon of August 10, the *Bear* began steaming north and east to Point Barrow through the drift ice. Her arrival at Barrow was delayed by more fog and ice.

No. 55. Trading and dance house at Icy Cape.

No. 56. Signal station at Point Barrow.

Barrow

Point Barrow was given its European name by Frederick W. Beechey in honor of Sir John Barrow, a second secretary of the British Admiralty (see Dease 2002). The point provided access to migrating whales, walruses, and seals, as was the case at Point Hope. There were several Native villages in this area, including Nuwuk, or Nuvuk, which Lt. Patrick Henry Ray, U.S. Army Signal Corps, had noted was much reduced by illness and starvation. Lt. Ray and his party were part of the 1881–1883 International Polar Year Expedition. Ray had set out for the western Arctic at about the same time as Adolphus Greely, who had led the Lady Franklin Bay Expedition, headed to the eastern Arctic with his party. Ray set up a signal station at Point Barrow in order to make meteorological, tidal, and magnetic observations (see Barr 2008).

On Friday, August 13, 1886, several men at the signal station were waiting for the *Bear*. In the spring and summer of 1886, Naval Ensign William L. Howard had successfully explored the area between Fort Cosmos, Lt. Stoney's camp on the Kobuk River in the interior of Alaska, and the Beaufort Sea to the north. Howard, from Norwich, CT, had entered the Naval Academy in 1877. He had been a member of the expedition that rescued Lt. Greely and his starving party in the eastern Arctic, who were desperately waiting for the relief ships that did not reach them for two years in a row. That relief expedition was the one in which the *Bear* took part in 1884. Ensign Howard spent the winter of 1885–1886 at Fort Cosmos with Lt. Stoney. He then headed north on April 12, 1886, with F. J. Price, a sailor; Riley, an interpreter; and two Natives. His detailed ethnographic description of the trip was included in Stoney's report published by the United States Naval Institute (Stoney 1899:811–822). Howard and his party hunted caribou and, driving fifteen dogs with two sleds, followed the upper Noatak River over the mountains. They then travelled down the upper Colville River to the Ikpikpuk River, threading their way to the Beaufort Sea east of Point Barrow. From there Ensign Howard and sailor Price made their way to Point Barrow on the ice, arriving on July 15, 1886. The two men went to the former signal station, which was by now under the command of Captain E. P. Herendeen and three traders employed by the Pacific Steam Whaling Company. On August 11, Howard and Price started down the coast to meet the whaling fleet, which was working its way eastward through the ice to Point Barrow. They found the *Narwhal* and were taken by Captain Millard back to Point Barrow to await the *Bear*, which was following close behind the whaling fleet.

From the Logbook

The *Bear* arrived at Point Barrow on August 13. Lt. Benham noted in the logbook that they

> Made out 12 vessels of the whaling fleet to Wd and saw the land to the S.E. 6 miles. Hauled up North. At 3.30 turned to N.E. for Meteorological Station at C. Smyth. At 4 made fast to the ground ice off station.

Between 4 and 6 PM there was a gentle breeze and the weather was clear. Lt. Dunwoody wrote that he

> Sent an officer to the station and brought off Ensign Howard and one man of the Stoney Expedition. Took a series of observations azimuth and altitudes + determined the variation of the compass to be East 32° 12' and Long. West 136° 50' 30". Signal Station bearing East 1'.

61 Steamer Bear in Ounalaska

No. 61. Steamer *Bear* in Unalaska.

The Bear Turns South
for San Francisco

The *Bear*'s first summer cruise had just reached its midpoint. On Sunday, August 15, the *Bear* got underway at 9:40 PM. The weather clearing, she turned west and then south, to pick up the leader of Ensign Howard's party, Lt. George Stoney, and the other members of the Naval Exploring Expedition at Kotzebue Sound. On August 26 she set a course for St. Michael, where Stoney's steam launch, the *Explorer*, was sold for $2,000 to Charles Peterson of St. Michael. The Native families who had needed transportation left the vessel with their effects. The crew brought coal inshore for the Alaska Commercial Company agent and the Episcopal missionary. Twenty-five miners came on board for transportation to Unalaska, having no other way to get there. The *Bear* left St. Michael on September 4, setting a course for St. Lawrence Island and then, on September 6, for Plover Bay, eastern Asia, where medical assistance was given to the Natives (see photograph 22). She patrolled the Pribilofs once again, stopping at St. George Island, where Lt. Hamlet made an official visit and Stoney's party and officers of the *Bear* made an unofficial visit.

On September 14 the *Bear* put in at Unalaska, where Third Lt. Benham noted in the logbook that he had been promoted to second lieutenant. The newly promoted lieutenant ended up serving on watch throughout that entire day and evening. The other officers seemed to have gone ashore, as no names appear on the cursory notations for the watches served for the next few days. The miners found temporary quarters and they also went ashore.

On September 18 Stoney and some members of his party also went ashore to wait while the *Bear* turned back to patrol the Pribilofs one last time. She was gone for eleven days, returning to Unalaska on September 30. The crew took on coal and water. Six seamen on the *Bear* volunteered to assist the captain of the *Memnon* to take her to Port Townshend, Washington, because some members of the *Memnon*'s crew were sick and incapacitated. The *Bear* took on six miners for passage back to San Francisco, "there being no other means of transportation." Eight members of Stoney's party were then transferred to work on the *Bear* to replace the men who went over to the *Memnon*. On Sunday, October 10, crew members started fires under the boiler in preparation for leaving Unalaska. At 2:05 PM they left the mooring buoy and steamed out of the harbor into a very heavy sea. They set course for Point Reyes, California. The *Bear* steamed and sailed south through ever-better weather. The crew scraped and painted.

The Bear *Comes Home*

On October 21, 1886, the *Bear* made land at Point Reyes. At 9 PM the *Bear* came to off the Washington Street wharf at San Francisco. The following day the miners went ashore and the starboard watch was given liberty. When the starboard watch returned from liberty on October 23, William Carey, boatswain, was not among them. The port watch then went on liberty, and Carey was discharged for being absent without leave. The next day the *Bear* arrived at the Mare Island Naval Base, near Vallejo, where Stoney and his party left the vessel. The *Bear* then returned to the Washington Street wharf. On the final day of the cruise, October 31, 1886, a coal passer, a seaman, an ordinary seaman, and a fireman were all discharged for drunkenness.

Some of the crew were to return to the Arctic the following year; others had had enough. As to the officers, Michael Healy continued as captain of the *Bear* until November 1895, when he was disciplined for his behavior toward officers and crew members and removed from command. Although he returned to service in 1900, he retired in 1903 and died the following year. The pallbearers at Healy's funeral were officers of the Revenue Marine Service, and former crew members of the *Bear* as well as captains of the Pacific Whaling Company fleet attended the service. He is buried in Colma, California.

Lt. Charles Kennedy returned to serve on the *Bear* in 1887 and was promoted to second lieutenant in February 1888, but he resigned in May of that year. The Kennedy family monument in New Bedford indicates that both his father and a brother died that same year, and that Charles Kennedy died in 1898. He was forty years old. Third Lt. Francis Dunwoody was promoted to second lieutenant on this cruise of the *Bear*, and to first lieutenant (temporary) in 1895. He was made captain sometime between 1901 and 1903, and then senior captain in 1911. First Assistant Engineer Horace Hassell was promoted to chief engineer in 1887, and became chief engineer of the *Bear* in 1889. He died in San Francisco in 1893, "the oldest chief engineer in the United States revenue service," according to the *San Francisco Call*, June 30, 1893.

Lt. Oscar Hamlet became captain of the *Bear*. He then served as superintendent of the Coast Guard Academy from 1895 to 1898. In 1906 he took charge of Revenue Marine actions during the earthquake and subsequent fire in San Francisco. His son Harry was to serve on the *Bear* and became commandant of the Coast Guard in the 1930s.

Now back in San Francisco for the winter, Captain Healy submitted the transcript of the logbook of the *Bear* to the Revenue Marine Division, writing:

> The foregoing transcript of the Journal of the US Rev. Str *Bear* of her northern cruise during the summer of 1886 is respectfully submitted. M. A. Healy, Captain U.S.R.M.

The *Bear* had successfully completed her first summer cruise. She was home for the winter, and preparations for her next cruise north were already underway.

While officers and administrators of the U.S. Revenue Service looked forward to a long career of the *Bear* in Alaska waters and Arctic seas, it is probably fair to say that few would have bet on another twenty-one years of patrol duty in the western Arctic. Those subsequent years saw reoccurrences of the same incidents encountered in 1886: the *Bear* and her crew commandeered illegal cargos, watched for illegal firearms possessed by or traded to the Alaska Natives, provided medical treatment for the Natives as well as seamen aboard whaleships and other vessels, and collected navigational data to upgrade charts. The *Bear* would be recognized as far more than a revenue cutter. For the next two decades, the former Scottish sealer was the symbol of the government of the United States of America in northern waters. And for the inhabitants of coastal Alaska, the islands, and easternmost Siberia, Captain Michael Healy of the *Bear* was the personification of that government.

References

Adney, Edwin Tappan, and Howard I. Chapelle. 1964. *The Bark Canoes and Skin Boats of North America*. Washington, DC: Smithsonian Institution.

Aldrich, Herbert L. 1889. *Arctic Alaska and Siberia, or, Eight Months with the Arctic Whalemen*. Chicago: Rand McNally & Co.

Allen, Robert C., and Ian Keay. 2006. Bowhead Whales in the Eastern Arctic, 1611–1911: Population Reconstruction with Historical Whaling Records. *Environment and History* 12:89–113.

Aquila Books. 2013. "Kobuk River Eskimo Seen at Hotham Inlet, Alaska" photograph. (http://www.aquilabooks.com/Catalogues/Catalogue%20208/WebsiteCat208.html). Retrieved October 15, 2013.

Baker, William Avery. 1977. The Design and Construction of Steam Whalers. In Bockstoce, John R., William A. Baker, and Charles F. Batchelder. 1977. *Steam Whaling in the Western Arctic*. New Bedford, MA: Old Dartmouth Historical Society.

Barr, William. 2008. *The Expeditions of the First International Polar Year, 1882–1883*. 2nd ed. Calgary: Arctic Institute of North America.

Bear. Logbook of the 1886 Patrol of the U.S. Revenue Service Cutter Bear. Washington, DC: National Archives. RG22. Microfilm.

Beechey, Frederick W. 1832. *Narrative of a Voyage to the Pacific and Beering's Strait, to Co-Operate with the Polar Expeditions; performed in His Majesty's Ship "Blossom"... in the years 1825, 26, 27, 28.* 2 vols. London: Henry Colburn and Richard Bentley.

Bixby, William. 1965. *Track of the Bear*. New York: David McKay Company.

Black, Lydia T. 2004. *Russians in Alaska, 1732–1867.* Fairbanks: University of Alaska Press.

Bockstoce, John R. 1986. *Whales, Ice, and Men: The History of Whaling in the Western Arctic.* Seattle: University of Washington Press in association with the New Bedford Whaling Museum, Massachusetts.

————. 2006. Nineteenth Century Commercial Shipping Losses in the Northern Bering Sea, Chukchi Sea, and Beaufort Sea. *The Northern Mariner/Le marin du nord.* 16(2):53–68.

————. 2009. *Furs and Frontiers in the Far North: The Contest among Native and Foreign Nations for the Bering Strait Fur Trade.* New Haven: Yale University Press.

Bockstoce, John R., William A. Baker, and Charles F. Batchelder. 1977. *Steam Whaling in the Western Arctic.* New Bedford, MA: Old Dartmouth Historical Society.

Bockstoce, John R., and Charles F. Batchelder. 1978. A Gazetteer of Whalers' Place-Names for the Bering Strait Region and the Western Arctic. *Names. Journal of the American Name Society.* 26(3):259–270.

Bockstoce, John R., and Daniel B. Botkin. 1983. The Historical Status and Reduction of the Western Arctic Bowhead Whale (*Balaena mystictus*) Population by the Pelagic Whaling Industry, 1848–1914. *Reports of the International Whaling Commission*, Special Issue 5: Historical Whaling Records, Cambridge, UK.

Brower, Charles D. 1947. *Fifty Years below Zero*: A Lifetime of Adventure in the Far North. NY: Dodd Mead. Note: Brower wrote several manuscripts concerning his life in Alaska before *Fifty Years below Zero* was published. Part of one manuscript was serialized between 1932 and 1934 as "My Arctic Outpost" in an adventure magazine, the *Blue Book*. The other manuscript was titled "The Northernmost American." The manuscripts, held in the Stefansson Collection at Dartmouth College, show heavy editing and excisions by editors, some of which removed Brower's colorful descriptions of people and events. Also, as Vilhjalmur Stefansson said in a 1947 letter to an acquaintance, editors also "jazzed" up the text of *Fifty Years below Zero*, rendering some of it inaccurate.

Burch, Ernest S., Jr. 1981. *The Traditional Eskimo Hunters of Point Hope, Alaska: 1800–1875.* Barrow: North Slope Borough.

Burch, Ernest S., Jr. 1998. *The Iñupiaq Eskimo Nations of Northwest Alaska*. Fairbanks: University of Alaska Press.

————.2005. *Alliance and Conflict: The World System of the Iñupiaq Eskimos*. Lincoln: University of Nebraska Press.

————.2006. *Social Life in Northwest Alaska: The Structure of Iñupiaq Eskimo Nations*. Fairbanks: University of Alaska Press.

————.2012. *Caribou Herds of Northwest Alaska*. Igor Krupnik and Jim Dau, eds. Fairbanks: University of Alaska Press.

Cook, James. 1842. *The Voyages of Captain James Cook. Vol. II. London: William Smith.*

Dease, Peter Warren. 2002. *From Barrow to Boothia: The Arctic Journal of Chief Factor Peter Warren Dease, 1836–1839*. Edited and annotated by William Barr. Montreal: McGill-Queen's University Press.

Elliott, Henry W. 1890. The "Lagoon" Rookery, with its Surroundings of the Killing Grounds, Landings, and Village of St. Paul's Island, June 6, 1890. http://en.wikipedia.org/wiki/File:NOAA_Saint_Paul_Island_elliott4.jpg. Accessed January 13, 2010.

Fienup-Riordan, Ann. 2005. *Yup'ik Elders at the Ethnologisches Museum Berlin: Fieldwork Turned on Its Head*. Seattle: University of Washington Press.

————.2007. *Yuungnaqpiallerput/The Way We Genuinely Live: Masterworks of Yup'ik Science and Survival*. Seattle: University of Washington Press.

Fitzhugh, William W., Susan A. Kaplan, and Henry B. Collins. 1982. *Inua: Spirit World of the Bering Sea Eskimo*. Washington, D.C.: Published for the National Museum of Natural History by the Smithsonian Institution Press.

Foote, Berit A. 1992. *The Tigara Eskimos and Their Environment*. Barrow, Alaska: North Slope Borough Commission on Iñupiat History, Language, and Culture.

The Fur-seal and Other Fisheries of Alaska. 1889. Report from the Committee on Merchant Marine and Fisheries of the House of Representatives. Washington: Government Printing Office.

Giambarba, Paul. 1967. *Whales, Whaling and Whalecraft*. Centerville, MA: The Scrimshaw Press.

Giddings, J. L., and Douglas D. Anderson. 1986. *Beach Ridge Archeology of Cape Krusenstern. Eskimo and Pre-Eskimo Settlements around Kotzebue Sound, Alaska*. Publications in Archeology 20. National Park Service, U.S. Department of the Interior, Washington, DC.

Graburn, Nelson H. H., Molly Lee, and Jean-Loup Rousselot. 1996. *Catalogue Raisonné of the Alaska Commercial Company Collection*. Berkeley: University of California Press.

Healy, Michael A. 1887. *Report of the Cruise of the Steamer "Corwin" in the Arctic Ocean, 1885*. Washington, DC: Government Printing Office.

———.1889. *Report of the Cruise of the Steamer "Corwin"in the Arctic Ocean in the Year 1884*. Washington, DC: Government Printing Office.

Hooper, Calvin Leighton. 1884. *Report of the Cruise of the U.S. Revenue Steamer "Thomas Corwin" in the Arctic Ocean, 1881*. Washington, DC: Government Printing Office.

Issenman, Betty Kobayashi. 1997. *Sinews of Survival: The Living Legacy of Inuit Clothing*. Vancouver: UBC Press.

Jackson, Sheldon. 1894. Report on Education in Alaska. Chapter XXV. Report of the Secretary of the Interior, Being Part of the Message and Documents Communicated to the Two Houses of Congress at the Beginning of the First Session of the Fifty-Second Congress, pp. 923–960.

Jarvis, David H. 1900. *Alaska: Coast Pilot Notes on the Fox Islands Passes, Unalaska Bay, Bering Sea, and Arctic Ocean as Far as Point Barrow*. Washington, DC: Government Printing Office.

Kaplan, Susan A., and Kristin J. Barsness. 1986. *Raven's Journey: The World of Alaska's Native People*. Philadelphia: University of Pennsylvania.

Kelly, John W., Sheldon Jackson, and Roger Wells. 1890. *Ethnographical Memoranda Concerning the Arctic Eskimos in Alaska and Siberia*. Sitka, Alaska: Society of Alaskan Natural History and Ethnology.

King, Irving H. 1996. *The Coast Guard Expands. 1865–1915: New Roles, New Frontiers*. Annapolis, MD: U.S. Naval Institute Press.

Larsen, Helge, and Froelich Rainey. 1948. Ipiutak and the Arctic Whale Hunting Culture. *Anthropological Papers, American Museum of Natural History*. Vol. XLI.

Lee, Molly. 1983. *Baleen Basketry of the North Alaskan Eskimo*. Seattle: University of Washington Press.

Lee, Molly, and Gregory A. Reinhardt. 2003. *Eskimo Architecture: Dwelling and Structure in the Early Historic Period*. Fairbanks: University of Alaska Press and University of Alaska Museum.

Lowenstein, Tom. 2008. *Ultimate Americans: Point Hope, Alaska, 1826–1909*. Fairbanks: University of Alaska Press.

Muir, John. 1917. *The Cruise of the* Corwin. Boston and New York: Houghton Mifflin Company.

Murdoch, John. 1892. Ethnological Results of the Point Barrow Expedition. Washington DC: Smithsonian Institution Press. Reprint 1988.

Nabokov, Peter, and Robert Easton. 1989. *Native American Architecture*. Oxford: Oxford University Press.

National Maritime Digital Library. http://nmdl.org/sfs/SFIntro.cfm. Accessed July 27, 2011.

Nelson, Edward W. 1877. SPC Arctic Eskimo Ak NM No # Nelson 01428700, National Anthropological Archives, Smithsonian Institution.

———.1899. *The Eskimo about Bering Strait*. Eighteenth Annual Report of the Bureau of American Ethnology for the Years 1896–7. Washington, DC: Government Printing Office.

Noble, Dennis L., and Truman R. Strobridge. 2009. *Captain "Hell Roaring" Mike Healy: From American Slave to Arctic Hero*. Gainsville, FL: University Press of Florida.

O'Toole, James M. 2002. *Passing for White: Race, Religion, and the Healy Family, 1820–1920*. Amherst: University of Massachusetts Press.

Oakes, Jill, and Rick Riewe. 2007. *Alaska Eskimo Footwear*. Fairbanks: University of Alaska Press.

Orth, Donald J. 1967. *Dictionary of Alaska Place Names*. Washington: U.S. Government Printing Office.

———.1970. North Slope Geographic Name Sources for Geologic Nomenclature. *Proceedings of the Geological Seminar on the North Slope of Alaska*, pages R1–R10. http://archives.datapages.com/data/pacific/data/028/028001/R1_pso2800R1.htm. Accessed January 22, 2012.

Papers Relating to the Foreign Relations of the United States. 1888. Washington, DC: Government Printing Office.

Powell, Eric A. 2009. Origins of Whaling. *Archaeology*, 62(1):27.

Pringle, Heather. 2008. Signs of the First Whale Hunters. *Science* 320:175.

Rainey, Froelich G. 1947. *The Whale Hunters of Tigara*. Anthropological Papers of the American Museum of Natural History, 41(2). New York.

Ray, Dorothy Jean. 1967. *Eskimo Masks: Art and Ceremony*. Seattle: University of Washington Press.

———.1975. *The Eskimos of Bering Strait, 1650–1898*. Seattle: University of Washington Press.

———.1981. *Aleut and Eskimo Art: Tradition and Innovation in South Alaska*. Seattle: University of Washington Press.

Ray, Patrick Henry. 1885. *Report of the International Polar Expedition to Point Barrow, Alaska, in response to the resolution of the House of Representatives of December 11, 1884*. Washington: Government Printing Office.

Report of the Commissioner of Fisheries to the Secretary of Commerce and Labor for 1885. 1887. Washington: Government Printing Office.

Ross, W. Gillies. 1985. *Arctic Whalers, Icy Seas: Narratives of the Davis Strait Whale Fishery*. Toronto: Irwin Publishing.

Smith, Barbara. 1984. Church of the Holy Ascension, Unalaska. National Register of Historic Places Inventory Nomination Form. (http://www.nps.gov/akso/cr/akrcultural/CulturalMain/2ndLevel/NHL/3PDF/70000112.pdf). Accessed October 29, 2009.

Smith, Philip Sidney. 1913. *The Noatak-Kobuk Region*, Alaska. U.S. Geological Survey Bulletin 536. Washington: Government Printing Office.

Stoney, George M. 1899. Naval Explorations in Alaska. An Account of Two Naval Expeditions to Northern Alaska with Official Maps of the Country Explored. U.S. Naval Institute Proceedings, vol. 25. September and December, 91:533–84, 92:799–849. Annapolis, MD: United States Naval Institute. http://tinyurl.com/y8pr2cr. Accessed December 29, 2009.

Strobridge, Truman, and Dennis L. Noble. 1999. *Alaska and the U.S. Revenue Cutter Service, 1867–1915*. Annapolis, MD: U.S. Naval Institute Press.

"Ten Days in the Arctic: The *Yukon* Cruising on the Alaskan Coast." *New York Times* December 6, 1880, p. 2.

U.S. Coast Guard Cutter History. *Bear*, 1885. http://www.uscg.mil/history/webcutters/Bear1885.asp. Accessed January 16, 2010.

VanStone, James. 1962. *Point Hope: An Eskimo Village in Transition*. Seattle: University of Washington Press.

————. 1989. Nunivak Island Eskimo (Yuit) Technology and Material Culture. *Fieldiana, Anthropology*, New Series 12. Chicago: Field Museum of Natural History.

VanStone, James, ed., 1977. A. F. Kashevarov's Coastal Explorations in Northwest Alaska, 1838. David H. Kraus, trans., *Fieldiana, Anthropology* 69:v–79.

Whalemen's Shipping List, and Merchants' Transcript. National Maritime Digital Library. http://nmdl.org/wsl/wslindex.cfm?year=1886. Accessed August 2, 2011.

Zagoskin, Lavrentiy. 1967. *Lieutenant Zagoskin's Travels in Russian America, 1842–1844. The First Ethnographic and Geographic Investigations in the Yukon and Kuskokwim Valleys of Alaska*. Henry N. Michael, ed. Arctic Institute of North America. Anthropology of the North: Translations from Russian Sources, No. 7. Toronto: Arctic Institute of North America.

Zimmerly, David W. 1979. Hooper Bay Kayak Construction. Canadian Ethnology Service, Mercury Series no. 53. Ottawa: National Museum of Man.

————. 2000. *Qayaq: Kayaks of Alaska and Siberia*. Fairbanks: University of Alaska Press.

Index

Note: **bold** page numbers indicate photographs.

121